goats eat cans
volume 2

STEVEN NOVAK

Published in the United States of America by Quiet Corner Press in cooperation with The Literary Underground, Yucaipa, California. www.litunderground.com

Copyright © 2012

All rights reserved. No part of this publication may be reproduced or transmitted in any form or by any means, electronic or mechanical, including photocopying, recording, or by any information storage and retrieval system, without permission in writing from Quiet Corner Press

Cover design and interior illustrations by Steven Novak

www.novakillustration.com

ISBN: 0615617824
ISBN-13: 978-0615617824 (Quiet Corner Press)

DEDICATION

For every crewmember of the USS Enterprise (NCC-1701-D) except Guinan. I hate you, Guinan

ACKNOWLEDGMENTS

It takes a lot of people to write a book. Wait, no, actually it only takes a single person with far too much time on his or her hands. It does take a lot of people to polish a book and make sure it doesn't suck, though.

A million thanks to my pals at The Literary Underground, and to MJ Heiser for agreeing to take her trusty red pen to yet another book of mostly nonsense and to Mary Ann Bernal for going above and beyond, and above and beyond that.

A million and a half thanks to my wife for not divorcing me after reading this. She could have. She probably should have. She didn't.

She either loves me very much, or she's sort of a dope.

Either way I'm reaping the benefits.

-Steven

LITTLE STEVIE PRANCE A LOT

LITTLE STEVIE PRANCE A LOT

My father is what is commonly referred to as a *man's man*. He always was and always will be.

I'm not even 100% sure what that's supposed to mean. I think it may have something to do with driving a large truck to compensate for a somewhat small penis, but don't quote me on that—otherwise a *man's man* is likely to kick my ass.

Growing up, my father absolutely loved his Sunday football. He loved fast cars that made lots of noise. He was physically attracted to metal. Screws gave him a boner. Nails brought him to the brink, and power tool put him over the edge. Things that made lots of noise, a cold brew, camping and the outdoors and fire and nature—these were his weekends and his weekdays, and the things he dreamed about when he was asleep. He had pictures of hot sluts in skimpy bikinis on the inside lid of his toolbox in the garage. If you were to give the man a hammer, he could add an addition onto your house.

If someone gave me a hammer, the most likely result would be me running around the room calling the hammer an asshole because it squashed my thumb.

Long story short, my father and I never really had too much in common.

Growing up, he was never that crazy about the drawing, or the writing, or the fact that I had very little interest in wasting my Sunday watching football.

As I got a little bit older, I think he was equally unimpressed with the fact that it took me until the age of 21 to send my schlong spelunking down a womanly hole.

A *man's man* would have scored long before that.

I can't imagine the old man was all that nuts that the woman I ended up marrying had a last name of Mexican descent either, but that's a whole other story.

Back in the days of Buster Browns, and operating under the assumption that all girls possessed a terminal disease sometimes called "cooties," my father loved to drag me fishing with him.

Fishing.

Fucking fishing.

I hated fishing.

Fishermen love to say things like, "I caught three fish today." No, you didn't, dumbass. The dead worm, the current and the hook did pretty much all of the work for you. Don't go getting too big an ego over that three-pound "monster" you reeled in with the strength of your gargantuan wrists.

I think my father believed taking me fishing at an early age would somehow counteract my love for crayons and pretty colors, maybe even save me from a life of ass-less chaps, KY jelly and a pair of balls slapping me in the taint as I took it from behind.

What's that you say? That doesn't make any sense? You've never heard that the best way to not be gay is to go fishing?

Really? Never? *Wow.*

Yeah, well neither did I. The old man seemed to believe it, though.

Ultimately, the problem was that every single trip ended the exact same way, which was precisely the opposite he would have wanted it.

We'd arrive on the banks of the Fox River early in the morning. I'd spend the first couple hours sitting, waiting, sitting some more, and then waiting a little bit more. Eventually I'd get tired of sitting and waiting, and I'd inform my father that I wanted to move further downstream. Believing that I had suddenly discovered some long-hidden love for fishing, he'd smile happily and wish me luck.

Here's the catch: Instead of moving further downstream to fish, I'd spend the next few hours examining the river banks for cool looking rocks and shells with pretty colors.

Yep, I typed *pretty*. Pretty is generally not thought of as a very "manly" word, but I typed it and I'm sticking with it. Deal with it, Pops.

Sticking with stuff is *manly*, right?

By the time I returned to where he was, I'd have a fish pail full of rocks where there was supposed to be a fish, and a very nerdy grin on my boyish face.

He would look at me, then the rocks, and finally back at me. "What were you doing over there?"

He already knew the answer to his question. He just couldn't accept it as reality.

I held the pail out in front of me and smiled like a goober. "Collecting rocks and stuff. See?"

His face scrunched like he'd just bit into a lemon, peel and all. His eyes went into a barrel roll so large that it would have made a fighter pilot jealous.

In that moment I could see him imagining me twenty years later as a fruity geologist in tan khakis and a goofy hat and cringing at the idea that every Christmas I might drag my life partner Brian with me back from San Francisco for a visit. Maybe we'd buy him some new drapes as a present and spend the afternoon complaining about the Republicans not wanting us to get married. Oh yeah, he was worried.

He was very worried.

Truthfully, I can't honestly say that he was thinking any of that, but I'll bet you a hand job it was pretty damn close.

A *manly* hand job, of course.

-Steven Novak-

I WAS A SCOUT

I WAS A SCOUT

On my honor, I will do my best. To do my duty to God and my country and to obey the Scout Law; to help other people at all times; to keep myself physically strong, mentally awake, and morally straight.

That's the official Cub Scout Oath. I'm amazed I remembered it, especially when you consider the fact that I have made no attempt to do any of the things they made me promise to do.

Maybe I've stayed mentally awake?

No, probably not.

I mean, can anyone who's watched episodes of the old *He-Man and the Masters of the Universe* cartoon on DVD really claim they've spent their years trying to remain mentally awake?

Orko simply isn't food for your brain, kids. Remember that.

I didn't love being a scout. I didn't even really like it. In fact, I hated almost everything about Scouting. I hated the camping. I hated the stupid crafts. I hated the badges. I hated the undeniably gay-looking outfit.

Let's speak frankly for a moment, shall we? That outfit was gayer than a gay guy in ass-less chaps and a leather vest, taking part in a gay orgy in the alley behind a theater in San Francisco where Liza Minnelli is performing—which is pretty gay.

Even at an age when girls weren't even interested in boys, they were somehow *less* interested in a boy sporting a navy blue shirt and matching short shorts. Oh, and let's not forget the yellow handkerchief. That handkerchief really finished off the ensemble.

The real reason I was a Cub Scout was that it got me out of the house for an hour and a half a week so my parents could splash around the water in their waterbed while they ground their genitals together.

Or maybe they would just yell and fight?

More than likely it was both.

Screw. Fight. Make-up. Screw again. Finish it off with a fight.

I think that pretty much sums up marriage, doesn't it?

Every week my mother would drive me across town where my "Pack" would meet in the basement of a church. She'd smile like a goof and say, "I'll be back to pick you up in a couple hours, Steven. Have fun."

I'd respond with something along the lines of, "Sure Mom, bye," but I was really thinking, *Fuck you. You want me to have fun? Take my pudgy ass out for ice cream. I've got about as much interest in making a Christmas tree out of acorns as I do in tying my hairless little boy wiener to a paint can utilizing the square knot I just learned and then trying to lift it.*

One of my fellow scouts was a kid named Tom Males. We sometimes called him Mayo, or even mayonnaise—neither of which made any sense. We were just kids though, so lay off.

As a joke I once told Tom that his favorite place to go was the male strip club "Mennigans."

Get it? Males, naked men—Mennigans? Sort of like Bennigans?

Fuck you! It got a pretty decent laugh back in the day!

Anyway, one night Paul, myself and a couple other scouts were outside the church after the meeting had ended. We were waiting for our families to pick us up and were leaning against a wall chatting about the one thing boys of all ages like to talk about: girls.

More specifically: boobs, and panties, and the butts wedged into those panties. Occasionally we would discuss their faces, but not that often. Oh, and sometimes we even talked about their minds and their sparkling personalities.

*Cough *I am a liar* Cough*

The conversation was going smoothly until Paul decided to chime in. "Hey, Steve, you know who I think is hot?"

"Who, Mayo?"

"Your mom."

What a little prick.

My mom? Where the hell did he come up with that? Can you believe the balls on this jar of mayonnaise, gay strip club-loving little shit!

"Shut up about my mom, Mayonnaise."

"Sure, I'll shut up — when your mom grabs my wiener and gives me a hand job."

Wiener? Hand job? What the hell? What's this little schmuck's problem!

"Say one more thing about my mom and I swear I'll kick your ass right here, Mayo. Don't push me."

There was a pause. Tom wasn't entirely sure if he should take it any further. I was quite a bit bigger than he was. Briefly, he looked down at his feet for answers. He dug his toe into the grass, considering his options, maybe searching for a way out.

After a minute or so of silence, he made his decision and responded with the first thing that popped into his head. "I'll lick your mom's boobs and sniff her bra."

Though it was incredibly stupid, for some reason the mention of sniffing my mother's bra made me snap. I let out a yell so loud that it made people with perfect hearing deaf, and for some reason made it possible for the hearing impaired to hear again. I charged at Paul, slammed my body into him and tackled him to the grass.

Almost immediately he grabbed my neck from the bottom and started to squeeze.

I returned the favor.

His fists started flying. He was punching me in the ribs from the bottom and I started punching back.

My knuckles smashed into his ear and he winced and screamed. "Oww! No punching in the ear!"

The punching stopped instantly. "Oops. Okay, sorry. No ear punching."

I didn't really want to get punched in the ear, so if that was going to be a rule, I figured I could roll with it.

Just as I was agreeing to the new fight format he punched me in the ear.

Little fucker!

The shot to the ear made me so mad that I was frothing at the mouth. The sounds coming from me were weird, gross inhuman things, loud and mean and nasty, like a pack of gorillas raping Jane Goodall.

While her hand gestures might have been saying no, *her eyes were saying* yes.

In a matter of moments I'd gone crazy! My general frustration with all things Scout and Scout-related was pouring through my fists and colliding with Mayo's face. I felt like Robert DeNiro in that scene from "Cape Fear."

You know which one I'm talking about: the one where he takes a bite out of Illeana Douglas's cheek and spits it onto the bed.

A few minutes later the pack leader was on top of us, trying to pry us apart while I'm screaming the words, "You wanna smell her bra now? Do you? You wanna smell her bra, Mayo? I'll smell *your* bra, dickface!"

I had absolutely no idea what that last part meant. I didn't really care.

After some wrangling, Mr. Thompson managed to pull me off of Paul, but I was still raging. Not entirely sure who was tugging at me, I threw a wild elbow and it connected with Thompson's piss stick.

He immediately grabbed his crotch and screamed like a twelve-year old girl — or Anakin Skywalker when he awoke for the first time in his Darth Vader garb. Inhaling deeply, he crumbled to the ground and coiled himself into the fetal position.

Needless to say, I was asked not to come to any more Scout meetings.

I wasn't that heartbroken.

When I got home my mother asked me why I got in a fight. I told her it was because of the smell of her bra.

She looked at me like I was an idiot. Because I was.

-Steven Novak-

CRUSTY POOP HANDS

CRUSTY POOP HANDS

Believe it or not, I often get asked the question, "Why do you have such an aversion to poop?"

I know. What a wonderful question to constantly get asked, right?

Other people get things like, "So how's work been? I heard you got a new promotion!" or, "Wow, where did you get that suit? That's mighty sharp-lookin', kiddo!" or even, "Have you lost weight, because you are looking fantastic!"

Me on the other hand, I get questions like, "Did that (*insert poop story*) thing really happen?" or, "Man, you really do hate poop, don't you?"

To answer the second one first, yes. Yes I do. I hate it a lot, in fact. I even hate poop more than I hate questions about poop.

I hate poop more than I hate Nazi Germany. I hate it more than I hate starving children. I hate it more than I hate a giant barrel of dead puppies. I hate it more than I hate the fact that the old Incredible Hulk television series was canceled so early on in its run.

Why do I hate poop so much? Well, when I was a kid–around six or seven years of age–I had this problem.

I was still shitting my pants.

I'm not completely sure why it was happening, but it was happening nonetheless. I can tell you without a doubt that I absolutely hated bathrooms. I hated toilets. I hated the guy who created toilets, even if I had no idea who in the hell he was. Instead of using them, I would sometimes just drop to one knee and sit my ass on my heel.

No matter how badly I needed to go, and even if it had been a week since I dropped a few logs, I didn't want to set foot in the bathroom, and because of that I had to plug the old poo-hole and keep the brown nastiness from squeezing out.

Essentially I was using my heel as a cork.

If that log was intent on coming out, it was not only going to have to force itself past my tightened anus and buttocks, but also have to squish itself around the barrier of my heel blocking the exit.

It seemed like a solid plan at the time. I know it sounds stupid, but it really did.

I just don't think I ever gave enough credit to the "squish and spread" abilities of feces. The poop moved through the cracks and the air pockets left by my heel with all the ease of Robert Patrick's T-1000 in liquid metal form. In doing so it coated my tighty-whities with sticky, chunky, nutty awfulness.

My parents were fairly disgusted with the whole situation, and with good reason.

Knowing they hated it, and fearing punishment, I would sometimes sneak my shitty poop pants out to the garage when no one was looking, open the garbage can, and stuff them deep down into one the bags.

While this worked for a while, my mother kept wondering what the heck was happening to all the underwear she was buying for me.

One day my father came into my bedroom with a pair of poop-crusted underpants dangling from his finger.

"I'm so sick of this shit, Steven. What the hell is your problem?"

How do you answer a question like that? Is there even an answer?

For the life of me I couldn't come up with a response that was going to make anyone feel better about any of it. Instead I said nothing.

"Well? What's the problem here, Steven? You are way too old to still be doing this! This is bullshit and I am sick of it!"

No pops, actually it's human shit. Bull shit *would be a whole different animal, and in far more copious amounts.*

Once again, what response was he looking for exactly? *I'm hoping to grow some prize-winning tulips for the state fair next month? It's fertilizer?*

He grabbed me by the arm and tugged me up so hard that for a minute I was almost weightless. I felt like one of the kids from that movie Space Camp, only with a sore arm, and having a lot less fun. Fuming, the old man pulled me out of the bedroom, dragged me through the hall, and into the bathroom.

"Every time you do this, from now on you're going to wash it yourself! With your hands!" He turned on the water, dropped my poopy pants in the sink, and motioned for me to get started.

Let me make this perfectly clear, my friends: there are few things as odd feeling as wet, human shit mixed with some lukewarm water on your skin. Don't get me wrong; while I'm sure there are a whole lot worse, washing your poop-laden pants is certainly near the top in weirdness.

I scrubbed at that thick-layered shit for twenty minutes, until it was completely gone and then hung my underwear over the shower to dry.

The best part of hand scrubbing shit comes long afterward when you discover the incredible amount of poo particles remaining underneath your fingernails.

Let's just say that I learned very early on to not bite my nails. As weird as poop on your fingers is, it's even weirder on your tongue.

I eventually stopped shitting my pants, but it had very little to do with my father's punishment. In fact, after a while I actually became very accustomed to the whole process of scrubbing my own undies and would even do it without even being told.

My father once walked into the bathroom and spotted me at the sink, scrubbing away at a particularly sticky patch of brown. He stared at me with maybe the most dumbfounded and disgusted look a man has ever had. "What the hell are you doing?"

"Just washing my underwear."

I confused my father most of the time.

I frustrated the hell out of him the rest.

MY FIFTEEN MINUTES OF SUCKY FAME

MY FIFTEEN MINUTES OF SUCKY FAME

Everyone gets fifteen minutes, right? That's what Andy Warhol said, isn't it? My issue is this: what happens if your fifteen minutes kind of suck? To be more specific, what happens if your fifteen minutes involves Bozo the Clown? Mine did.

When I was just a wee tyke with a pair of still hairless nuts tucked safely inside some of my mother's famous homemade shorts, and a gap in my mouth where my two front teeth once resided, I used to watch Bozo. Every day. Religiously.

That red-haired freak was my cocaine. He was my heroin, and my crack, and my sugary breakfast cereal all rolled into one. He was my addiction, and it wasn't until I discovered boobs that he was replaced.

In my hometown, Bozo aired on the "Superstation," WGN. Yep it seemed all you had to do to be called a "Superstation" was to show re-runs of I Love Lucy, the Ray Comb's version of Family Feud (pre-suicide of course), and Bozo the Clown.

I'm not even sure that Bozo is around anymore, but when I was the kid, this guy was the absolute *shizznit*. I'm talking ol' school gangsta-clowning here, you know what I'm sayin'?

Minus the gangsta, of course.

The show taped out of the city of Chicago, and somehow my parents got hold of some tickets. You have no idea how excited I was. Seriously, you can't even begin to contemplate my level of anticipation.

Pretend you've been abducted by a race of ultra-sexy, big-boobed space aliens who happen to be from a planet where all the men have died off. You've been abducted and chosen as the lone male to help them repopulate their planet. Imagine all those space-legs you'll be spreading—and all the alien genitals you'll buried in.

Imagine all of that, multiply it by two, and you're getting just a little bit closer to the excitement I felt about going to see Bozo live.

Also, just for kicks, take the number you got above and divide it by thirty-four, and toss in three hundred million. Why? I don't know. Just do it. I think it would be funny to watch you try and do the math.

While waiting outside the studio before the show, my parents were approached by one of the show's producers who asked them if I'd like to participate in one of the games.

My mother turned to me. "Steven, do you want to pla—"

"You better believe I do, you damn wacky bitch!"

Okay, so maybe I didn't say *exactly* that to my mother, as she would have smacked me in the face if I had. I did however offer up an extremely excited "Yes!" while jumping up and down like a twelve year-old girl with a tingly crotch coming face to face with Justin Bieber.

For those of you out there somewhat familiar with the Bozo show, don't cream your shorts in jealousy just yet. I wasn't actually going to be playing the ping-pong ball into the buckets thing that the show was famous for. No, I was set to take part in one of the smaller games earlier in the show.

Still incredibly cool by the standards of any seven year old out there, but not Steve McQueen cool like the buckets game would have been.

This was more like Bruce Willis cool.

Well, Bruce Willis-Sin City cool, anyway. Not Bruce Willis-Hudson Hawk cool, which honestly is more like Anything Done by Ashton Kutcher cool. Which isn't very cool at all. (I've put way too much thought into this, haven't I?)

About fifteen minutes into the show, myself and five other kids from the audience picked to participate were led onto the stage.

From a removable wall to the left of us, a long wooden plank with paper cups on the top of it was rolled out. Bozo's sidekick and whipping boy, Cookie waddled over and handed each of us a little water gun.

Six kids all lined up, across from them eight cups per kid, and sixty seconds to try and shoot as many of the cups off the plank as you could with your little water gun. The winner would get a prize. This was the game.

I squeezed the handle of my little green plastic gun, and steadied my stance. I was so gonna win this.

I briefly glanced at the kids on either side of me. They were nothin' but a bunch of scrawny wimps. Meager-looking arms, candy on their faces, messy little kid hair. Nothing but pussies and wimps and wimpsies; I was going to murder them.

I looked in the direction of the cups across from me. I squinted my eyes and tightened my jaw. These fucking things were going down. They were going down big time. They were going down like a frightened teenage girl going down for the very first time.

They had no idea what was coming.

In my mind, at that moment, in the company of the blue-suited, red-haired, red-nosed god among children, Bozo, I was going to have a moment that would define my life forever. I was going to do something the kids at school would be jealous of and something that would make those damn cootie girls look at me in a completely different and slightly confusing way.

We're talking life altering, *more important than the return of the Savior Himself* stuff here, people.

I raised my gun and steadied my arm. I took a deep breath and held it.

Bozo looked us over. "Are you ready for this, kids?"

For a moment I could have sworn he was talking and looking specifically at me, that he was challenging me.

Let's do this.

"Theeeeennnnnn goooooo!!!"

I took down those cups like I'd trained half my life in the military as a sniper. I kid you not. Ten seconds flat. It was amazing. It was more than amazing. It was so amazing there isn't even a word for it.

It was so amazing that the people in the audience that day undoubtedly expected me to spin the pistol around on my finger, hold it to my mouth and blow smoke from the barrel. Maybe even spot off a corny, horribly written, action film-esque catch phrase like, "Looks like somebody couldn't hold their water."

Bozo rushed over to me, grabbed my wrist and held it up. "We have a wiiinnneeerrr!!"

No doubt he was thinking to himself *damn, that kid can shoot!*

What was my prize for winning on the Bozo show?

Optimus Prime.

That's right, Optimus Prime: the leader of the Autobots, assholes. Maybe not as overall cool as Soundwave, but still extremely fucking cool.

This truly was the greatest day of my life.

Jealous much?

If you are, you really shouldn't be. Turns out as dumb as it was for me at the time to think this would be the absolute high point of my life, that's exactly what it ended up being.

Seriously, it was downhill from there.

Now excuse me while I go cry into my pillow, hug Optimus Prime, and remember when I actually mattered.

THE EIGHT YEAR-OLD KILLING MACHINE

THE EIGHT YEAR OLD KILLING MACHINE

When I was young, in the days before pubic hair, chest hair, facial hair, and yes, unfortunately, ass hair, I had a friend named Scott.

Scott was what my mother called a "bad influence," and what my father called a "stupid piss-ant little fucker."

Dad always had such a way with words, sort of like Bill Cosby mixed with Charles Bukowski.

One day Scott suggested that we hide in a row of trees across the street from a neighbor's house and throw some rocks at it.

Why?

I don't know.

The house was there. The rocks were there. I guess in Scott's mind the two just went together like peanut butter and jelly or Maury Povich and a fifteen-year- old who's been tested fifteen times and still hasn't found her *baby's daddy*!

I knew that it wasn't exactly in my best interest to lob rocks at people's houses. I was dumb, but I wasn't an idiot. What I didn't really have much of was a little something called common sense. For some reason, even something as stupid as chucking rocks made perfect sense in my confused little brain, and before I knew it I was crouching down into the brush next to Scott, grabbing a handful of rocks and tossing.

Some slammed into the siding. Some hit the door. One hit a window and left a sizable crack from the top to the bottom. For ten minutes we just kept whipping stones, and laughing and ducking down, blissfully unaware of the fact that someone was apparently inside: someone who decided to call the cops.

When a cop car came rushing around the corner, we jumped and scattered. Scott ran off in one direction and I hurried in another.

My choice of directions took me straight into a cornfield.

My legs were pumping and my chest heaving. Not once did I look back. I couldn't. I just ran and kept running, as fast as my somewhat chubby, eight year old frame could manage.

Which honestly wasn't that fast. Try to picture a drunken camel huffing its way through the desert with wads of spit flipping from the corners of its mouth. That was pretty much me.

Then out of nowhere, WHAM!

I was knocked on my ass.

Standing above me was a local cop, dressed in blue and wearing one of those belts with a bunch of crap on it.

He was also sporting a fairly hilarious-looking mustache.

This dude was the real deal.

You see, apparently I'd ran right into his legs.

How pathetic is that?

It's more pathetic than that time Don Johnson released an album in the 1980s.

My criminal career was over long before it had even begun. Not only was I never going to be Clyde, I wasn't even Bonnie, or Bonnie's grandmother, who had cancer, and as far as I'm aware, never robbed shit.

The cop helped me up, walked me to his car and threw me in the back. A quick drive later we were parked outside my house, and I sat in the back watching as he approached the front door to talk to my parents.

The whole thing was supposed to scare me, I think. Even at eight-years-old I knew I wasn't going to get arrested or end up in jail, even if that's what he wanted me to believe. While the cop explained to my father what had happened, I looked in front of me and noticed that he'd left his shotgun within reach.

Almost instantly my boyish mind went crazy with possibilities. Oh, the things I could have done with that gun—the wonderful, wonderful things.

I could have shot my way out.

Yeah, that's it; shoot my way out. Grab that gun, use it to blow open the door, hop out and go to town on this fucking cop!

I pictured myself running around like a madman, jumping over cars and shooting in all directions. I could see myself doing a couple cool spin-kicks, somehow getting my hands on a pair of ninja blades and flipping through the air like, Michael Dudikof in *American Ninja*.

Back up would be called in and I'd take them out as well.

"So what's the situation, Jackson?"

"Well sir, we've got an eight-year-old kid…waitwaitwait, I know it doesn't sound like much, but damn it, he's good! He's fast! Too fast! He's spinning around and doing flips! Donaldson over there has a ninja-star in his forehead! We ju—"

"He's an eight-year-old kid, Jackson!"

"Maybe so sir, but this is no ordinary eight-year-old kid. This kid's a killing machine."

The army would be called in and I'd head into the mountains like John Rambo from *First Blood*. Covered in dirt and camouflaged with the surrounding forest, I'd take them out one by one — dance in their blood and wear their intestines as a scarf! I'd be unstoppable!

Yeah. This was going to be so damn cool.

I'd teach that cop. They'd never try and stop me from throwing rocks again.

All I had to do was grab that gu—

The car door opened. The cop pulled me out. He led me to the front door of my house by the collar of my shirt and deposited me at the front door. Once inside, my old man screamed at me, told me to drop my pants, pulled off his belt, and gave me one of his world famous bare-assed whuppins.

There was no back up, no army and most definitely no hiding in the woods, setting traps and picking people off one by one.

John Rambo I was not.

I was barely John Wilkinson — and I don't even know who that is.

In the end I was just some pudgy kid with a really sore, really red ass.

I once made a cardboard ninja-star though. I guess that was sort of cool.

-Steven Novak-

THE GAME WE CALLED COLLEGE

THE GAME WE CALLED COLLEGE

"So, what do you wanna do?"

That was me.

"I dunno."

That was my best friend, Eric.

"Me either."

"College?"

"Play college?"

"Yeah, sure. You want to?"

"Yeah, okay."

We were about eight-years-old at the time and, as you've no doubt gathered from the exchange above, we called the game *college*.

Most of the time, Eric and I spent our time together collecting bugs or building forts, or pinning dead bugs to the walls of our forts. On the rare occasions when bugs and forts weren't enough to cut the mustard - or just when the weather sucked - we would generally fall back on *college*.

I know exactly what you're thinking. *What the fuck is college? If this son of a bitch types the word* college *one more time and has the unmitigated gall to put it in italics without telling me just what in the hell he's talking about, I'm going to shove my hand down his throat, grab his intestines, pull them through his mouth, and wrap them around his neck like a jaunty little scarf.*

First things first: You're awfully violent.

Second things second: To make a long story short, the game of "*college*" basically consisted of, Eric and I hanging out in my bedroom, talking to each other and acting out what we imagined our lives would be like when we grew up and found our way to college.

It was simple and it was sort of gay.

When I say gay, what I really mean is lame – the sort of gay that has absolutely nothing to do with becoming aroused by the wonderfully lucid smell of man ass.

Most of the time, anyway.

What's that? You think the game of *college* sort of, kind of, maybe just a little bit sounds like something a couple of girls might do? You think it has a lot in common with pre-teen pigtailed females bouncing around in their bedroom acting out situations like meeting a hunky guy, or getting married, or having a big beautiful wedding and somehow inexplicably becoming a princess?

Well, if it sounds like a *girlish* sort of thing for a couple of young boys to do, that's because it was.

The only major difference between what we were doing and the games of our penis-less counterparts was that I don't recall Eric or I ever fantasizing a *college* scenario in which we donned a pretty pink dress and married a dashing young prince in a flowered gazebo near the ocean.

Well, wait.

I guess there was that one time.

The thing both amazing and pathetic about the game of *college* was the type of situations we seemed to think would regularly happen to us once we came of college age.

We expected loads of women and mountains of booze. We anticipated an endless parade of parties, and piles of crotchless panties – some filled with drugs and others were filled with the more traditional female genitals.

Maybe even a few filled with both.

An afternoon of *college* would generally begin with Eric sitting on my bed, basically chillin' with just a little bit of illin' — *you know, like college kids do.* He'd pretend to hear a nonexistent phone ring and promptly pretend to pick up.

"Hello? Yep, this is Eric. Oh, hey Shannon. Yeah. Sure. What are you up to? Oh, really? Yeah. I think we can do that. Totally awesome. Sure. Yeah, see you then, sexy."

In the pretend world Eric was a smooth-talking pimp with a game so big it could hardly be contained. In the real word he was sort of a weirdo – and a dork – and sort of gross.

Eric pretended to hang up the pretend phone and turned to me with as lecherous a grin as an eight-year-old could possibly muster. "Guess who that was?"

I was sitting on the pretend bed at the opposite end of the room in our pretend dorm. I rubbed my hands together like a cartoon villain and smiled. "Shannon?"

"Yep."

"What did she want?"

"She's on her way over."

"No shit?"

"Yep, and she's bringing Debbie."

"Radical!"

Yeah, that's right, I said radical.

Don't judge me too harshly, though. I was only eight and the Ninja Turtles were popular at the time. Everything was either *radical,* or *bodacious,* or *totally tubular.*

We immediately scampered to tidy up our pretend dorm and make it somewhat presentable for the visit of our pretend and no doubt ample-breasted college cuties.

I knocked twice on the wall with my fist. "They're here."

After making my way to the pretend door and pretending to open it up, I stepped to the side and let in the pretend girls. As I pretended to watch them pass by I also pretended to look at their pretend butts, and pretended to mutter the word *"dayyyymmmm"* silently to myself in my pretend imagination.

Wait - enough of this.

Pretend imagination? *Isn't that basically the same thing?*

I really need to stop typing pretend.

I'm not going to though.

I should, but I'm not going to.

It's amusing me to no end.

Every time I do it, I chuckle to myself.

Eric and I pretended to spend the next ten minutes sweet-talking the girls. Mindless small talk, even pretend mindless small talk, ended up getting really old, really quick, and before we knew it we'd removed the shirts of our pretend female companions and were pretending to cop ourselves a pretend feel.

The Muppet Babies used to pretend like this. Minus the boobs, of course.

Not long afterward we'd managed to get their pretend everything off, and soon after that the orgy was underway.

Eric was propped up on his hands, staring at the bed underneath him with a truly terrifying grin and humping the air at a ninety-degree angle.

Taking a moment from pretending to give it to my pretend girl-toy doggie style, I spotted Eric out of the corner of my eye and felt the need to speak up. "It wouldn't work like that."

"What do you mean?"

"It wouldn't work. A real pussy isn't on top like that. You need to do it on more of angle." In order to show him what I meant, I flipped over my pretend girl, placed her pretend legs on his shoulders, rotated my hips and began to hump the air.

It was disturbing.

My know-it-all bravado also annoyed Eric. "How do you know where a pussy is?"

"Everyone knows. It's obvious."

"Shut up."

"You shut up."

"No. You shut up."

"You shut up infinity."

"You shut up infinity plus one."

"Fine. Do whatever you want, but when the time comes to actually get it on with a girl at college you're gonna feel pretty stupid."

Out of the many, many things wrong with the situation as a whole, this was the one I chose to point out.

Seriously?

That's just stupid.

In time I'd come to the awful conclusion that the craziest notion we had while playing *"college"* was that the women in college would call us and ask to come over - or for that matter, talk to us at all.

The pussy placement predicament was the least of our problems.

PROVE IT, LIAR

PROVE IT, LIAR!

There are moments in a life when a select few are able to take their meager existence and advance it to the next level.

Rosa Parks did it when she refused to give up her seat on the bus.

Neil Armstrong did it when he became the first human being to ever set foot on the surface of the moon.

Michelangelo Buonarroti did it when he completed his work on the Sistine Chapel.

Phil Collins did it when he released the timeless *Sussudio*.

Paris Hilton did it when she banged that one dude on videotape.

In the vein of these champions of human betterment, I too have played a part in one these life-changing escapades.

Want to hear about it?

No?

Too bad.

"Shut up assmunch! You don't have pubes."

That was my friend, Derek. His finger was poking me in the chest, his face barely three inches from mine and his voice was louder than normal. He was making sure that each one of our five or six friends in his mother's backyard heard him clearly. He wanted everyone to understand beyond a shadow of a doubt that he didn't believe a word of the outlandish claims I'd just made. His hands were airborne, every gesture dramatized. He was being obnoxious. He was forcing me to respond in kind.

And respond I would.

Let me backtrack for a second, though.

As is often the case with young boys, moments before Derek so defiantly rose to face me, the conversation between the six of us had turned to girls, and sex, and *wieners*, and pubic hair. To be more specific about it, we'd begun discussing whether or not any of us had actually grown any.

Our friend Matt was the first to speak up. "I've got a ton of hair down there. It's like a forest, or something."

We all knew he was lying. We could read it in his body language and see it in the look on his face. Derek was the only one of us that chose to call him out on it. "Shut up. You don't have anything down there."

"Yes I do."

"No you don't. You're lying."

"I do."

"Prove it."

"I'm not gonna prove it, Gaylord. I'm not showing you my pubes."

"That's cause you're a liar and you don't have any. None of us do yet. I'll bet you like…five thousand dollars that I get them before any of you dorks do!"

Matt returned to his chair with a huff. He lowered his head like a puppy that pooped on the carpet and had his snout rubbed in it. He'd been defeated. Derek called his bluff and in doing so, Derek had won.

Believe it or not, I liked Derek. In fact, it would be fair to say that he was my *best* friend at the time.

He was also a bit of an asshole.

He liked to push people around. If he wasn't the center of attention, he wasn't happy. He was the class clown, the loud mouth, the braggart. He was confident in that frustrating way only a child that hasn't yet been trampled on by the realities of life can be. Everyone knew a Derek growing up. Derek was the sort of kid that needed to be put in his place, even if only once.

The question was, who among the small group of friends hanging out in his backyard talking about the raisin-chested girls at school would have the guts to stand up to him?

Because my friends were, for the most part, losers, it looked as if the task would fall squarely on my shoulders. I was the last option and the last hope — a bastion of hope amidst a sea wickedness. I was the final solution. Like Keanu in the Matrix, I was *The One*.

Someone needed to put Derek in his place. He was just asking for someone to stand up to him, and I was confident I had the skills necessary to do exactly that.

When I say *skills* in this case, I'm of course referring to the mildly impressive peach-fuzz that had begun to sprout in around the general area of my crotch a few months earlier. Which is sort of a skill. No?

Shut up. It's a skill.

Let me pretend it's a skill.

It makes the story sound cooler if it's a skill.

I steadied my legs and puffed out my chest. I crossed my arms, lifted my jaw and focused my gaze singularly on the task at hand. This was it. This was the moment. After taking a deep breath I let the words spill from me like a hero's speech moments before the climactic scene in an action film. "I've got some pubes."

Rosa Parks would have been proud.

Derek stood up and moved toward me. "Shut up, assmunch. You don't have pubes."

"Yes I do."

"No you don't."

"Yes I do."

"Liar."

"I know you are, but what am I?"

Awesome comeback.

"Prove it."

This was the moment of truth, the instant in which the men were separated from the boys–literally–seeing as pubes were involved.

"Fine." I stood up and started to unbutton my pants.

Initially Derek was surprised by my eagerness. His surprise quickly turned to anger. Someone was standing up to him. It was a classic case of the old *switcheroo*. For the first time in a very long time, someone was calling his bluff. My friends leapt to their feet and formed a circle around me. Their eyes moved to my crotch as I started to unzip.

While I didn't whip out my little boy junk and start flapping it around, I did pull my pants down just enough to show off my crotch grass.

It was short – a bit paltry looking if I'm honest – kind of like the green on a golf course.

Short or not, there was no denying the fact that it was pubes.

A sort of airy, noiseless-noise emerged from the group of gap-jawed onlookers. It was layered in shock, slathered in awe, and drenched in bewilderment. On the top of it all was an Emeril-sized *BAM!* of jealousy.

Did I just make an Emeril reference?

The problem was, with everyone staring at my crotch, no one heard Derek's mother approaching from behind. Suddenly she was standing above us, peering down into the group of boys and trying to figure out what the hell was going on. "What are you boys looking at—"

She spotted my fuzz. Spotted me showing off my fuzz. Spotted five kids staring down at my fuzz.

I can't imagine what the poor woman was thinking. It must have all seemed gayer than Doogie Howser in a three-way with Clay Aiken and Tom Cruise at a gay brothel in the fictional city of Gaytown, Gayklahomo.

Which would be pretty darn gay.

Her first reaction was to scream. "Oh my God! What the hell are you doing?"

The group scattered in every direction.

Derek and two kids slid into the house. Another ducked behind the shed and hopped over the fence. Two more headed for the street where they ran and continued running until they got home.

I tried to zip up my pants, but my shirt got caught in the gears of the zipper, which made it almost impossible and also tossed me off balance. I was half trying to run and trying to zip at the same time, while having very little success at either. Instead I was just spinning awkwardly in a circle.

I glanced at Derek's mother. She was staring at me like I'd just transported down from my mother ship with a pair of wobbly antenna bobbing atop my head, like I was a weird little thing from another world that she wanted nothing to do with.

I stumbled into one of the patio chairs, flipped over it and was suddenly rushing toward the ground. I landed hard on my right shoulder, smacked my nose against the concrete and bruised my thigh.

Derek's mother tried her best to keep herself from laughing.

She failed.

Her hand went to her mouth and her eyes began to water. Trying to hide her face, she made a weird snorting noise before scampering into the house.

My shoulder hurt like hell.

There was dirt in my mouth and my pants were around my knees.

I looked like an idiot.

I did have pubes though, and that's worth something.

Right?

YOGI BEAR CAN KISS MY ASS

YOGI BEAR CAN KISS MY ASS

I hate camping and I hate Yogi Bear.

I guess I'm sort of indifferent to Boo Boo Bear, but that's a whole other story for a whole other time.

When you put camping and Yogi together you get the *Yogi Bear Jellystone Park Campground*, which I also hate. My parents used to drag my brother and me to this awful bastion of all things civilized and respectable every year when we were kids.

I still don't see what we were supposed to like about this place.

Maybe the mosquitoes?

How about the community showers? Oh, yeah, those were a blast and a half.

Was it the outdoors? How about the act of sleeping on the ground in a rain-soaked, foul-smelling tent? The hillbillies? The *S'mores*?

Actually the *S'mores* weren't all that bad.

If you discount the *S'mores* though, camping plain old sucked. Thanks, but no thanks. Sorry, that sort of nonsense just wasn't for me.

It never was and it never will be.

If you're the kind of person who happens to love that sort of thing, awesome. Coolio. Good for you, you crazy camp-loving son of a bitch. Go sit by the river for five hours and catch a fish for dinner if you want. I'm sure it'll taste delicious when it's been infused with all that campfire goodness. I'm ordering a pizza. It'll be delivered to my door in thirty minutes or less, I'll be done eating it in thirty-five and asleep in thirty-seven.

Despite my incessant bitching, the vast majority of the camping trips I was subjected to as a youngster were, for the most part, completely forgettable.

Except for one.

For the trip in question, my father allowed both my brother and me to bring along a couple of our friends.

This was of course back in the days when I actually had friends, back when I was fully capable of engaging other human beings in conversations without freaking out, wetting my pants, and frantically searching for the nearest bridge to jump off of.

I invited my pals, Derek and Jimmy, to come along. If nothing else, I figured that just having them around would make the trip somewhat easier to handle and walk away from with my sanity in check.

At the time, it seemed like a fairly solid piece of logic.

Like most things in my life, however, it was doomed to failure. It was going to backfire and it was going to leave me as pissed off as a female porn star who took the money shot in her eye instead of on her boobs.

It was going to backfire so badly that the backfire backfired on the backfire.

Shut up. That makes perfect sense.

After arriving at the campground, parking in our lot, and setting up the tent that Derek, Jimmy and myself would be spending the night in, we noticed something especially interesting about the family in the lot next to ours.

They were a family with a daughter around our age.

They were a family with a girl around our age, who also happened to bring along two of her friends.

They were a family with a daughter around our age, who also happened to bring along two of her friends, and all three of them were hot.

Well, as hot as eleven year-old girls that haven't grown boobs and are barely sporting cooter fuzz can be, anyway.

Jackpot!

That's what we'd hit! The fucking pre-teen booty jackpot!

Note: Between you and me, that was an exceptionally awkward sentence to type. I just want you to know that I'm not proud of myself for doing it. It was necessary and it serves the story, but it was still weird.

It's also the sort of thing that can land me in jail with some guy named Roscoe working himself up my keyster if interrupted the wrong way or taken out of context.

By the end of the first day we found ourselves with the three of them in their camper after the adults had left for the pool. We were talking and laughing, and awkwardly flirting, despite having no real idea what the term *flirting* actually meant.

The short girl with the dark hair in the ponytail licked her lips, crossed her legs in her tiny little shorts and smiled at me in a way that made my mouth dry and my pants fit uncomfortably. "So are you guys going to the stupid dance thing tonight?"

For the life of me, I can't remember her name. I wish I could, but I can't. Maybe it's because I had spent most of the conversation staring at her legs and very little actually listening to anything coming out of her mouth.

I think that might have something to do with it.

The dance was at the entertainment center near the park entrance later that night, and immediately Derek's voice cracked out a "Fuck yeah!" in response to her question. He then proceeded to tell her that we'd meet the three of them there.

Derek was a player. He knew what he wanted, and what he had to do to get it. He was an eleven-year-old suburban white-boy pimp without the feather hat.

Me on the other hand, well, I was just a putz. I was fairly positive what I wanted; I wanted those legs. I just had no idea how to get them. I was the opposite of a pimp.

Dancing, going to a dance, dancing with a girl: these things scared the piss out of me.

Why couldn't she just let me feel her up and be done with it? Why did I have to jump through hoops? I would have happily allowed her to juggle my boy balls around for a bit if she really wanted to. All she had to do was ask. I certainly wouldn't have required her to do the *running man* thing in a public place while a C&C Music Factory song blared in the background to get a crack at them.

Hours passed and night rolled around. Suddenly it was mere minutes before we had to leave for the dance. Decision time.

You already know what I did, don't you?

Yep, I did what any wormy little girl-boy would have done in the same situation: I told Derek and Jimmy to go without me.

I punked out.

I threw in the towel before the game even began. I folded before I had any cards. I ate sushi when what I really wanted was a burger. I sat through an entire episode of the Real Housewives of We Should All Be Shot, and never once pointed out the fact that they were possibly the most awful people in the history of history's history.

If my father had seen me do it, he would have called me a queer, shoved some lunch money in pocket, punched me in the gut, pushed me over, and stole it right back.

If I'd had a breezy little summer dress with me, he might have told me to put it on.

Maybe even a cute little gardening hat to finish off the ensemble.

And you know what? I'd have deserved the humiliation.

I simply could not bring myself to do it. I just couldn't. Their faces and their legs and the way their legs moved when their faces did stuff—it was too much for me to process.

In the end, Derek and Jimmy went without me.

Thirty minutes later I found myself sitting alone on a bench near the empty baseball field in the dark. From off in the distance the song "*More Than Words*" by the band *Extreme* filled the night air.

To this very day I still fucking hate that song.

I also still hate camping.

And I hate Yogi Bear.

I despise most females, pre-teen or otherwise.

And of course, I can't stand myself.

I guess I'm okay with Boo Boo though. Boo Boo has never done me wrong.

LİTTLE KİDS SHOULDN'T SHAKE LİKE THAT

LITTLE KIDS SHOULDN'T SHAKE LIKE THAT

Anyone who's around my age no doubt remembers the wildly pathetic *Lip Sync* craze of the 80's, right?

Everybody was doing that nonsense. They were doing it in bars, and cars. They were doing it in their houses, and with their spouses. They were doing it in full-on costumes in the — um...

Bostrooms?

Shut up. It's hard to rhyme with costumes.

If memory serves, I believe there was even a short-lived game show on television that featured the musically untalented doing it for modest cash prizes. It was annoying. It was stupid. It wasn't really fun to anyone, anywhere, unless you were drunk or *special*. If you happened to be one of the unlucky many forced to watch it, you wanted to kill the morons doing it.

Guess who was one of those morons?

Tom Selleck.

Of course it wasn't Tom Selleck, you idiot.

It was me.

You see, when I was in the sixth grade my school had a *talent show*. Myself, and my friends, Derek and Andy, decided we'd enter and do a little *Lip Syncing* of our own.

I know, I know, it's hardly worthy of the word "talent." I'm aware of this. Pretending to sing and dancing around like an idiot is hardly worthy of a pat on the back and a "good job, son" from an old man in checkered pants, but whatever. When in Rome, right?

If the country falsely believed it took talent to pretend to impersonate someone with talent, who was I to argue?

Of course, the rest of the world also thought, Emilio Estevez was a *movie star* at the time. Look how that turned out.

My pals and I decided we would *perform* a song called *Up all Night* by the popular 80's hair band, Slaughter. We borrowed a drum set from Andy's older brother, lugged the electric guitar I never learned to play out of my closet and spent nearly three weeks *practicing* our routine and getting the timing down.

I even managed to put together a pretty sweet costume.

Pair of ripped, stone washed jeans? Check.

Black headband? Check.

Stupid looking, multi-colored strings tied around my arms and legs? Check.

Sparkles? Double-Check.

Hair spray? Checkity-check.

Black driving gloves? Check Into Cash.

Bright gold belt? Richard Speck.

Slightly feminine black jacket with shoulder pads that I stole from my mother's closet? Kiss on the neck.

Ultra tight, leotard-esque half shirt that allowed my pudgy grade school belly to hang out? I like typing the word *blech*.

Oh, when I said that I put together a *pretty sweet* costume a bit earlier in the story, it should be apparent that what I actually meant to type was *flamboyantly Liberace-gay* costume. *You probably already guessed that, didn't you?*

The day of the show arrived and the three of us trotted out onto the stage like we owned the place. I think I might have even winked at one of my female classmates.

In truth, we looked like complete tools.

We were walking with such confidence, though, that it was almost impossible to ignore us. We were glowing. We were hot and we were on top of the world, and we were moments away from rocking that gymnasium. We were Sean Combs and his posse, on their way into a club on a Friday night.

We were awesome.

The house lights dropped.

Because Mrs. Zimmerman, the kindergarten teacher nearest to the switch, clicked them off.

The intro to the song started to play and almost instantly the noise of the crowd lowered to a whisper.

The strobe lights we'd set earlier in the day came on.

Because, Mr. King, the music teacher, turned them on.

Moments later a guitar riff blared and the song kicked into gear.

Suddenly I was running from one end of the stage to the other and shaking my head like a crazy person. At one point I even slid across it on my knees. I popped up and set into a series of disturbing leg kicks and rolled into an unexpected somersault that garnered its fair share of *oohs* and *ahhs* from the crowd. I was nailing every single word. I was on point and I was sharp as a knife. I wasn't missing a beat.

Basically I was *Lip Syncing* the crap out of that song.

I shit you not, people, I was that damn good.

I was displaying the raw energy of a young Axl Rose, oozing with the sexual tenacity of a big-donged Tommy, and soaking in the undeniable dorkiness of the Nelson twins!

At one point I even snagged a handful of my little boy wiener through my jeans and give it a rub while humping the air.

More than a couple of the teachers weren't too nuts about this.

I dropped to my stomach and start humping the stage.

Maybe not so surprisingly, that maneuver didn't sit too well with them either.

Little boy ass, crotch and hips shouldn't have been allowed or capable of shaking like they were shaking. It wasn't right. It spat on the very laws of the universe and kicked gravity right in the testicles. There was something wholly unnatural about what was happening on that stage, like flying a kite in the dark, or the fact that Star Jones and *E.T.* look scary similar.

The performance was prime pedophile material, the sort of stuff your local pastor keeps in the *special box* under his bed.

Some parents were laughing. Some were completely disgusted. Ashley, the girl I had a crush on, sitting ten rows back, seemed to like it, though. Honestly, she was the only I really gave a crap about anyway.

The song ended, the lights flickered on, and almost immediately every kid in the crowd erupted in cheers.

To top it all off, though I was nearly out of breath, I managed to scream, "Thank youuuuuu, Crystal Lake Soooouuuuuth!"

For a single moment in time I felt like Jon Bon Jovi. In this briefest of instances, I was Sebastian Bach. For this millisecond of time, I'd transformed into Vince Neil, or to a much lesser extent, Kip Winger.

I was a superstar.

Sure, I was a superstar who had to drive home from the big show in his father's Rabbit, crammed into the seat with a drum set digging into his ribs.

Still a superstar, though.

-Steven Novak-

WHY DON'T WE LET STEVE DECIDE?

WHY DON'T WE LET STEVE DECIDE?

Divorce is a weird thing. Wait, no, actually, forget I said that and allow me to rephrase: Divorce was *once* a weird thing.

These days, it's about as common as a paparazzi snapping a shot of some Hollywood socialite's mommy mound as she steps out a limo.

In case the verbiage escapes you, I'm sure as hell not talking about a pregnant belly. Go a little further south.

Follow the scent of tuna.

I'm not one of those people who think divorce is necessarily a bad thing, and I definitely don't believe that it's single-handily going to be responsible for the fall of western civilization.

As luck would have it, that too can be blamed on bimbo socialites and their mommy mounds. Go figure.

The truth is that some people are just not meant to be together. It's really as simple as that. Sure, maybe things started out great and maybe marriage made sense at the beginning, but people change, and when people change, things change. Before you know it, you're lying across from someone you no longer recognize and the only thing you can think of is how much their breath smells like dog plop.

It probably sucks being married to dog plop and only dog plop.

Honestly, I was just about everything but upset when my parents decided to call it quits on a marriage in the summer before I entered the sixth grade. Their marriage was a disaster at that point.

It was a bigger disaster than those seventies, Irwin Allen flicks combined – including *Beyond the Poseidon Adventure*.

My parents' divorce meant I'd no longer have to lay awake at night listening to them argue. It meant I wouldn't have to spend my mornings listening to them argue, or my afternoons, or my nights.

They weren't just arguing, either; they were arguing about the same old shit over and over and over again. It was maddening. They were like ten-year-olds. They were like a couple of Tickle Me Elmo dolls being squeezed by some annoying little brat you know is fully aware of the fact that it's pissing off everyone around him.

Stupid brat. I know what you're thinking. You may have fooled them, but you aren't fooling me.

Money. Sex. Work. Friends. Kids. Sex. Money. Sex. Money. Kids. Money. Kids. Money. Kids. Kids. Sex with kids.

Okay, I made that last one up.

The whole situation was absurd, more absurd even then the fact that Ashton Kutcher had somehow managed to work regularly in Hollywood for over a decade.

My mother and father were two people who just needed to get the hell away from each other. Unfortunately for them, they had a pair of kids, and this is where things got sticky.

Word of advice for human beings everywhere: don't reproduce. There are enough of us running around as it is and we're pretty much all dicks.

The world doesn't need any more dicks.

Anyway, my parents now found themselves having to figure out things like: where do the children go? Who do they live with? Who gets custody? Who gets the house?

The house comes with the kids, right?

Cause I want the house.

I mean, the kids. I want the kids. Of course I want the kids...if they come with the house.

At the very least I don't want you to have them.

So how did my parents eventually decide to answer the most unanswerable of questions? Like their parents and the parents of the parents before them, they did what was easiest of course. They let someone else do it for them.

And that someone was me.

That makes perfect sense, right? I mean, who better to make massive, life-altering decisions than a ten-year-old kid? Right? No?

Of course not.

There are lot of reasons why there's never been a pre-teen president.

1. He or she has never really heard the term *intern*, and is only vaguely familiar with the specifics of a blow job.

2. He or she would more than likely choose to bomb Canada because Canada called him or her a homo and wouldn't return the *Starscream* action figure he or she let Canada borrow last week.

So there I was, a human being not quite old enough to have sprouted hair in the area around my arm pits, chest or genitals, dressed up in my Sunday best, standing in a dimly lit judge's chambers and sweating more than Michael Richards at a 50 Cent concert.

A million thoughts were running through my head. What the hell was I doing there? Why did my parents want me to talk to this guy? I thought they said that this divorce had nothing to do with me? And if it had nothing to do with me, why did I suddenly feel like it had a whole heck of a lot to do with me? Why did G.I. Joe's resident big man, Roadblock, always feel the need to talk in rhyme?

"We got a bargain, but play it straight or there's no doubt, I'll turn your eyeballs inside out"

What the hell is that even supposed mean, 'Block?

The room smelled like old people, like old people and their old asses. It was stuffy and sweaty, and just plain weird, sort of like a chicken taking a bath in a warm bowl of chicken soup.

It smelled brown, if brown had a smell.

The judge entered through the doorway over my shoulder and lowered his roundish body into the chair behind the desk across from me. He breathed deeply, looked right at me and shook his head before breathing deeply again and tapping his pen on the desk a few times.

After that, he just stared at me.

In a weird way, he sort of resembled Wilford Brimley. I was pretty sure I wasn't there to get lectured on checking my blood sugar and checking it often, though.

"Hello, Steven."

"Hello."

"Do you know why you're here?"

"Not really."

"Your parents thought it might be a good idea for me to talk to you and get your thoughts on who you think you and your brother should live with now that they're going their separate ways."

God damn it! So that was why my father took me out for ice cream without my brother last week! That was why my mother finally bought me those *Ninja Turtle* figures I'd been bitching about for a month!

Those tricky, tricky assholes; they were buttering me up. They slathered me like a piece of freshly toasted bread and dropped me on the breakfast plate.

I thought about the judge's question for a bit and answered as best as my ten- year-old brain could answer. When it was all said and done the person I picked was the exact person we ended up living with.

Of course, it was the wrong choice. And of course, the results were disastrous.

Years later I asked my mother why she and the old man felt the need to put that kind of decision on me. Her response was simple.

"Well, I don't know. It was a tough decision, Steven."

Indeed it was.

Now spread you legs a little because I'm wearing steel-toed boots, my kicking leg is stronger than ever, and I want to give you a hysterectomy.

-Steven Novak-

AMOS, ANDY, AND THE CORPSE OF KIP WINGER

WHY DON'T WE LET STEVE DECIDE?

Halloween is a kickass holiday when you're a little kid.

Dressing up in stupid costumes, going door to door to get free candy, then returning and filling yourself full of so much sugary goodness that your shit glitters like the dress of a Walt Disney princess—*yep, nothing beats Halloween.*

As fun as Halloween was in the days when underwear was still referred to as "big boy pants," it got progressively less fun around the time pubes started to grow in.

I'm not entirely sure of the science behind it; I haven't crunched all the numbers, or worked out all the angles, but I have a theory when it comes to the sprouting of hair in the groins of human beings. Are you ready? Okay, here goes.

Pubes equal jackass.

Impressive, huh?

And you thought the Masters Degree in "Science and Stuff" that I have hanging on my office wall was just something I picked up at a novelty shop in the Wisconsin Dells.

For me personally, when the scraggly patch of hair sprouted to life around my droopy Pinocchio, I decided I was way too *cool* to ever take Halloween seriously.

The days of getting wide-eyed and gushy over a fun size Snickers were gone for me. They were a distant memory and they weren't coming back.

"Fun size Snickers? They're *fun size* because they're for babies! Which means Halloween is for babies! Babies don't have crotch grass! I have crotch grass, so Halloween isn't for me!"

Believe it or not, I said something very similar around the time and believe it or not, it actually made sense.

With my new found hatred for all things Halloween and baby-related, I asked my friends, Derek and Jimmy, to join me on a quest to make Halloween, and all the stupid babies and their stupid fun size Snickers, pay!

Once again, believe it or not, I actually thought this, and it also somehow made sense at the time.

Derek brought over a tube of black makeup he'd stolen from the local store and we covered our faces in it. Since there wasn't enough makeup to go around, Jimmy snagged himself an old skeleton mask with long white hair from his basement and threw it on.

We looked sort of like Amos, Andy, and the corpse of Kip Winger.

Wait just one minute: is Kip Winger dead?

Oh well. If he's not, he might as well be.

I wouldn't have called our outfits "costumes" as they were our "anti-costumes." We were rebels, and we were doing whatever the hell we wanted to do! Common sense and consequences be damned! We were playing by our own set of rules and walking the razor's edge! We were teetering on the brink of life and de—

Sigh, I'm going a bit over the top with this, aren't I?

Yeah, I am. Sorry about that.

Sometimes I get worked up and don't know when to stop. My rants are just like Will Smith's career.

Honestly, we were little more than a few foul-mouthed, bored, trash-tastic D-bags with too much time on our hands and testosterone swimming around in our nuts.

(I'm not sure on the science of that.)

We were such little douchebags that we spent the vast majority of the evening going from house to house, snatching pumpkins off of the doorsteps and smashing them on everything from driveways to mail boxes and even the occasional cars.

When you throw a pumpkin against the hood of a car, the pumpkin itself doesn't technically end up "smashed" as much as the car is dented or the windshield cracked.

I suppose that's just a matter of semantics, though.

As the night began to wind down, we spotted a group of four girls we recognized from school. Two of them were dressed like witches and I suddenly had the overwhelming urge to find out if a witch's nipple is really as cold as the legend claimed.

Not far from the girls were a couple of younger boys we also knew from school.

You see where this is going, right?

Take some unsuspecting dorks, toss in a handful of hot pre-teen booty, sprinkle in a dash of stupid boys with the desire to impress and touch the previously mentioned booty, and you've got yourself a recipe for disaster. I'm talking about a disaster worse than the Tyra Banks talk show — and that was fairly disasterrific.

Derek looked at me and said two words, "brown wash."

That's all he had to say. I instantly knew what he was talking about. Jimmy knew what he was talking about.

It was game time.

Jimmy and I charged immediately at the dorks. I wrapped my hands around one of them and tackled him to the ground. While Jimmy and I were busy pinning his arms to his sides, his friend took off running.

The kid underneath us struggled to squirm free. He wiggled and wormed and tried desperately to free himself from the cackling idiots on top of him. He was screaming and yelling like a madman.

Unfortunately the only people within shouting distance were the booty girls, who responded by giggling at his misfortune.

Derek moved over the boy, dropped his pants (then his big boy pants), wrapped his butt cheeks around the poor bastard's face, and blasted a fart so loud that it could have woken the dead.

It sounded a little squishy, too. There may have been some leakage, or at least a brown mist.

If you're really starting to hate me right about now, it's okay. You should. It was a mean thing to do and I'm a terrible person for doing it.

If it makes you feel any better the next few years would be rough for me, really rough. By the time I got to high school the tables had turned and I was getting picked on mercilessly.

Karma is a son of a bitch.

SHAMEFUL ACTS AND BROKEN MICE

SHAMEFUL ACTS AND BROKEN MICE

I was sort of a weird kid growing up.

When I say *weird,* I don't just mean *odd,* either. It's not that simple.

I was screwed up.

There were some things that occurred after the divorce of my parents, things I don't generally like to talk about. (Maybe I'll work up the nerve to get into it for Volume 3.) Without a doubt, these unspoken things certainly contributed to my personality at the time, but that was only part of it.

I really was fucked up.

I mean fucked up on royally fucked up levels. I was royally fucked up like the corpse of Princess Grace of Monaco, being used as a toilet by a gang of homeless winos in surprisingly dapper checkered pants.

As luck would have it, it was also an idea for a script Hitchcock had bouncing around in his brain after wrapping "To Catch a Thief."

No wonder she quit acting.

There really is no way to sugar coat it. I was creepy-weird and I was scary-weird, and a little creepy-scary-weird on top of that.

Like I said earlier, sure, I could take the easy way out and blame it on my somewhat warped surroundings at the time, but that's essentially a cop out.

Some people are stranger than others and I was one of those people.

To this day very I'm still a bit of a weird sack of weird layered in a spicy weird sauce and coated with a crisp KFC crust. Compared to where I was, however, we're talking night and day, or lunch and dinner, or gay and straight, or dead and alive, or bearded and finely shaven, or racing stripe and clean, or flat as a board and rounded like the Rockies, or Rocky Balboa and Glass Jaw Jackson, or even The Muppets and Fraggle Rock.

Back then I was bordering on serial killer weird. If things had gone a different way, or I'd zagged when I zigged, who knows? You might have one day seen me on the news for slicing open heads and scooping out brains.

It's a fact that many serial killers came from abusive, screwed up households. It's also a fact that many of them suffered head injuries at some point in their youth. Nearly all of them were recluses who spent their lives unable to connect with other human beings on even the most basic of levels.

That makes me three for three. *High five!*

Oh, it's also fairly common for serial killers to have killed at least one small animal at some point while growing up.

Can you see where this is going?

At this point feel free to stop reading if you must. You can throw this book in the trash or delete it from your e-reader of choice, move to another state, change your name, and pray that I never find you.

Don't worry, you wouldn't be the first, nor do I imagine you'd be the last.

It's story time, kids.

I was twelve-years-old and I was sitting on the back porch of my childhood home. It was a sunny day. The sun was sunning and the birds were birding. It was warm, but it wasn't too warm. It was Goldilocks warm. It was a perfectly unassuming, completely pleasant, totally normal mid-western afternoon in every conceivable way.

It was practically an episode of the Brady Bunch, and it was the sort of day when families throw barbeques or pack up the kids and head down to the lake for a few fun-filled hours of swimming, good times, and the occasional awkward moment that comes when obese Uncle Teddy does a cannonball into the water, loses his trunks and pops up with his junk flopping in the wind like a tiny hairless Mogwai.

It's a perfectly nice, perfectly de—

Gah!

What the hell?

A tiny mouse scurried past my leg before leaping onto my hand and causing me to hop off of the porch and into a standing position screaming like a petite little lady on her first day as a porn star.

I turned around just in time to see the furry little jerk high tail it into a crevasse between the porch and the back of the house. Acting on instinct, like a cop chasing a perp or the previously mentioned porn actress chasing an STD, I hotfooted it after the little guy.

There was no way out of the area he'd gotten himself into. It was blocked at both ends.

I had him. I had him right where I wanted him. I had the squeaky, tiny-footed, jumping on people's hands and causing them to tinkle their britches little jerk.

He fucked up and he was mine!

A sick, demented smile stretched its way across my face, the sort of smile the invisible man smiles when he's hanging out in the high school girl's locker room, intermixed with the sort of smile Jeffery Dahmer made every night after dinner as he picked pieces of fingernail from the spaces in his teeth.

With a truly pathetic sense of pride and accomplishment (despite having done nothing to achieve either) mixed with a weird almost vampire-like blood-lust that was clouding my better judgment like a puff from the world's biggest bong, I came to a decision.

It was a crazy person's decision, but it was still technically a decision.

I spotted a wedge of wood lying next to the porch and snatched it up. Breathing heavily, I lumbered toward the trapped, fuzzy little creature like a cave man stalking his first meal, or Michael Jackson stalking little boys.

My hair was wild, my chest was heaving, and my eyes were twisted into a terrifying V.

In a movement so quick it made The Flash himself jealous, I lurched forward and pressed the sharp end of the wood against the spine of my tiny, helpless enemy.

I heard a crunch.

Despite this, I pushed down harder until his legs splayed straight and began to flail, until his eyes grew so large I thought they would pop from his helpless little skull.

His tiny vocal chords produced the teensy tiniest of blood curdling screams as his delicate spine snapped, crackled and popped like a bowl of Rice Krispies on the breakfast table of the devil himself.

It was amazing how long he took to die.

I could have stopped at any time, but I didn't.

Instead I kept pushing, and twisting, and grinding until I had nearly sawed him in half and a slimy, gooey mess of wet red and black had formed a puddle around him like something out of an Eli Roth film.

When it was over and he'd taken his last sweet little mousey breath, I reached down, grabbed hold of his tail, lifted his lower half into the air and drank from the warm elixir that one resided inside his veins.

Okay, so I didn't really drink his blood. That last part was a lie.

You believed it though, didn't you? For a second you did. *Admit it.* I mean, after everything you read before that, would it really have been all that crazy?

Truthfully, after it was over with, I felt nothing but shame.

I felt shame for what I'd done and for who I was letting myself become. I felt shame for breathing in the same air the rest of the non-mouse killing world breathed in so regularly. I felt shame for hurting something smaller than myself and doing it for no reason, beyond the fact that it was smaller, and I could.

I pretty much hated myself.

If one day I'm passing by a construction site and I'm chopped in two by a falling beam, don't feel too bad for me.

Karma is a very mean, foul smelling son of a bitch with terrible Mario Batali sausage farts.

Somewhere in the world beyond ours there will be a tiny chopped in half mouse, very deservedly laughing his furry little ass off. When I get there to meet him, he's going to bite me on the nuts.

And I'll deserve it.

PEN MAN

PEN MAN

I really do love drawing. It relaxes me, it takes my mind off of things, and it can make me feel like I've accomplished something on those days when I accomplish almost nothing at all. I've been doing it for as long as I can remember and I can't imagine that I'll stop anytime soon.

Drawing has gotten me into trouble on more than a few occasions, though.
It's gotten me kicked out of class. It's angered family members and drawn my attention away from important things like school, loved ones, and bettering myself as a person.

Drawing is like booze for me. It's easy to get caught up in and it's even easier to get lost in. Granted, I've never woken up in a naked puddle of pencil shavings with no memory of what I did the night before, but still, you get the point I'm trying to make, right?

For example, in one of my grade school science classes, my teacher asked the students to bring in something from home for an experiment we would be conducting the following week. He suggested that a baseball might work, or a basketball, or even an apple – basically something roundish - something that could be easily rolled.

I honestly don't recall the specifics of the experiment or what we were testing and more than likely this is because I didn't care.

I was a terrible student.

I was a worse student than Dr. Phil is a therapist. I was a worse student than Casey Anthony was a mother. I was a worse student than Dom DeLuise was a sex machine.

The following week, most everyone in the class managed to bring in something roundish, and something capable of rolling: most everyone except my friend, Mark.

To put it bluntly, Mark was a bit of a dunderhead (yep, I typed the word *dunderhead*), and Mark forgot to bring something in at all. With nothing available, my dunderheaded pal opted to try and roll his pen.

He failed miserably.

And I mocked him mercilessly for it.

The pen flipped and plopped and occasionally slid, but it never really came close to something anyone might consider a roll. It was a pathetic display. It was a pathetic display put on by a pathetic young lad, and he deserved everything I tossed his way.

Just when he thought I was done making fun of him, I decided to make him the lead character in a comic book called Pen Man.

In no time at all, my little seven-page joke was making its way around the class. My friends liked Pen Man. The class liked Pen Man. They liked the drawings, and they appreciated that it was poking fun at Mark.

A few of them wanted a copy, so I made some photocopies and sold them for a buck each.

Not long after that, they were clamoring for a second issue.

The character of Pen Man had become so well known that people started referring to Mark as Pen Man. Like nicknames tend to do, Pen Man stuck. In fact, people were referring to Mark as Pen Man more than Mark, which of course annoyed him to no end.

When I moved away a few years later, I kept on drawing Pen Man.

I don't really know why I did it. Mark was no longer a part of my life and I was at that age where selling homemade comics to people at school would have succeeded only in getting me beaten up.

"You like drawing comics, nerd? Then you're going to love drinking toilet water."

Characters from Pen Man spun off into their own titles, new characters were created, and soon enough my little brother (who came up with a few characters of his own) and I had created Novak Comics.

I know, it's a pretty creative name, right?

Well into high school, I was still drawing Pen Man. I drew him at home. I drew him on the bus. I drew him in the library. I drew him at lunch, and I drew him in class, continuing my legacy of truly awful studentry.

I know "studentry" isn't technically a word. Shut up. No one asked you. Keep your damn mouth shut.

Now, you might think I would have eventually stopped scribbling on typing paper in my free time and stapling the pages along the edge, but I didn't.

When I should have been soaked in booze and buried to the hilt in lady parts in college, I was still drawing Pen Man. When I should have been going on dates, and meeting women, and applying for jobs, and planning my future, I was still drawing Pen Man.

When I graduated, moved to California and got married?

Yep, I was still doing it then, at least for a little while.

Eventually I wised up and put the kibosh on the adventures of Pen Man and the whole Novak Comics thing as a whole. It was hard to do, but it had to be done. By that time I'd probably drawn well over five hundred issues, which is sad, terrifying, and just a tiny bit impressive, in a sad and terrifying sort of way.

For years since, the Pen Man books have been gathering dust in my office. The paper is crinkling. It's turning yellow, and it's getting brittle. Even the staples are beginning to rust. These things weren't made to last, and because of that I spent the better part of a year scanning and categorizing every single page of every issue. I even started to put them online.

I couldn't just let Pen Man rust away. Too many things go away in life.

Pen Man didn't need to be one of them.

There's a part of me that hopes Mark is still out there somewhere and he'll somehow stumble onto them during a break in his regularly scheduled internet porn routine.

Maybe, for the briefest of moments, he'll remember how much he hated it when everyone called him Pen Man, and he'll curse my name through clenched teeth.

That's the kind of stuff that brings a smile to my face.

LESSONS LEARNED, MILES WALKED

LESSONS LEARNED, MILES WALKED

For a brief period of time in junior high, I was an amateur wrestler. *The problem is that I wasn't a very good one.*

While I was relatively big for a seventh grader, I wasn't a *good* sort of big. I was beefy and I was spongy. I was doughy. I was round. I was a sloppy sculpted representation of a thirteen year old Lou Ferrigno made entirely of mashed potatoes and butter-soaked chives. My size was more a hindrance than anything.

It was clear to pretty much everyone that I'd been genetically gifted in certain respects, but I also had absolutely no idea how to utilize it.

I was sort of like the kid from that terrible, sappy Sandra Bullock flick about the feisty southern woman who saves the African American kid from a life of certain disaster (because everyone knows it takes a mouthy white woman to put things right).

Ahem. Cough. *Loadofcrap.* Cough. Ahem.

I just needed for Dolly Parton to believe in me.

With no real *skill* of which to speak, I was forced into the role of a *scrapper*. Scrapping I was good at.

If there was one thing I was more than capable of doing around that time, it was taking a beating. I could take a beating with the absolute best of them, and did quite often.

During my stint with the wrestling team, my face was mashed into the mat more times than I could count. *Seriously, my math grades were terrible.* My arms were twisted, and my neck was bent, and my legs were folded in directions human legs should never have been folded.

I think I might have once kissed my own ass cheek. *It had a surprisingly peppermint twang.* This might have had something to do with the fact that it was January and I was still farting Christmas.

Anyway, I was coiled, and mashed, and ground to a pulp, but I never once gave up. No matter how badly I was losing, or how many times I heard my spine snap or my bones pop, I was never pinned.

I took pride it that.

You see, my home life was sort of a mess at the time. Things weren't great when my parents were married, but they certainly weren't as bad as they would become after they were divorced. The situation went from bad to worse and it wasn't likely to get better anytime soon.

Wrestling eventually turned out to be a nice little escape. It was helping me deal with my anger, and while a part of me hated going to the practices, and getting screamed at by the coach, and pushing my tubby torso and jelly legs to their limits in constant, repetitive cardio and strength routines, another part of me was slowly beginning to like it.

It was certainly better than being home. At least I'd chosen those beatings.

By the end of the season, believe it or not, I was actually getting a little bit better at the actual "wrestling" part of wrestling. Sure, my body still wasn't doing what it needed to do, and I still wasn't winning any matches, but I was slowly transforming into something other than a tackling dummy to be used and abused like a crack sweat hooker with a brain that's more meth than gray matter.

I was fanning my anger positively. I was starting to learn how to use it. I was a becoming a werewolf, and my canines were transforming into fangs.

Unfortunately I was still a girlish, girl-obsessed, thickheaded, mostly dumb, hipster pants-wearing *Twilight* werewolf—but I was werewolf all the same.

With the final meet of the year approaching, I trained harder than ever. Not only did I want to win, but I was also starting to believe I might have actually had a chance of doing it.

I didn't complain even once when I was told to run the stairs. I didn't shake my head in frustration when reprimanded with a round of push-ups. At practice I listened closely to the coach and absorbed every word spewing from behind his mustached lip. I began to work certain escapes and situations out in my head. I trained them over and over on the mat. My muscles were beginning to remember. Suddenly they were reacting without me having to tell them. I was getting stronger. I was getting faster. My seventh-grader body was like a steel-coated cobra with a belly full of venom. It was coiled and it was anxious and ready to strike!

Okay, maybe steel is a bit of an overstatement. Maybe my body was more like a plastic rattlesnake. *At the very least it bared a passing resemblance to a tin foil gardener.*

Quite surprisingly, the night before the meet, my father told me he was going to show up. I didn't want him to. He hadn't been to any of them up to that point, and honestly he hadn't been missed. I told him that it wasn't necessary. He told me to shut up. Not only did he insist on going, but he also said that he would be driving me home afterward.

Damn it.

I tried to put it out of my mind.

It was a worry I didn't need, not when so much was on the line. I needed to focus. I wanted to win and I was ready to win. I'd put in the hours of work necessary. It was time to make it all worthwhile. I had to win. I needed to win. My life was a mess and I needed for something to go right. I wasn't going to lose.

I wouldn't lose.

I couldn't lose.

At the weigh-ins, I stared at my opponent from across the locker room, bared my teeth and might have even growled. The poor sap didn't know what he'd gotten himself into. Sure, he had a better record than me, and was better built, and probably stronger, and certainly a hell of a lot faster. So what if he'd been wrestling since he was eight-years-old, and wrestling was one day going to earn him a college scholarship and a spot at the Olympic trials. So what? That didn't mean shit! Dude was screwed. Dude was about to enter a lion's cage. Dude was a bloody slab of taut gazelle meat and I was hungry for dinner. *Dude was gong to get eaten alive.*

Guess what? Dude didn't get eaten alive.

Dude actually beat me.

Don't get me wrong; I didn't get my ass creamed like the finely-toned booty of a porn starlet after an hour on set. I held my own and it was the best I'd ever wrestled. When I was pushed, I pushed back. I sprawled and grabbed, and twisted and spun. Instead of trying to simply survive, I was looking to win, and it paid off. I scored points, and for a moment I swear I could almost see a hint of worry in his eyes.

I left everything I had on those mats. I emptied the reserves and emptied the reserves of the reserves. I gave it my all and then I gave it a little bit more.

In the end, it just wasn't enough.

After shaking hands and returning to the welcome embrace of my team, I started to cry. To this day I'm not sure why I did it. I had never been much of a crier and I'm still not, despite having had my fair share of opportunities to do so.

Plain and simple: I was emptied and I didn't have anything left.

I guess it had to happen sooner or later.

My chest started heaving, my eyes started to water, and once it was happening, I couldn't hold it back. My team patted me on the back and told me not to worry about it. The coach said it was okay and that I'd done a "hell of a job."

He was right.

When I looked up into the stands, I saw my father shake his head, curse under his breath and walk away. I took my time getting dressed. I languished in the locker room and thought about all the things I'd done wrong and the things I could have done to win. A half hour later, after everyone had already headed home, I discovered that my father hadn't just left the auditorium so much as he got in his car and drove home.

Damn it.

That night I walked home. It was a good six-mile trek and it was snowing.

Yep, that's right. I'm the guy who will one day be able to tell his grandkids that he actually had to walk home six miles in the snow and not be lying about it.

Oh, and I didn't have a coat.

So that was pretty awesome.

SARCASTIC DIXIE CUPS

SARCASTIC DIXIE CUPS

When I was in junior high, my mother and her boyfriend took my brother and me to a horseracing track a few cities over. Racetracks are undeniably interesting places.

There are horses. There are little men in checkered shirts, and tight pants that leave very little to the imagination. There are degenerate, broke ass gamblers. There are also a few degenerate, loaded ass gamblers. There are also a hell of a lot of degenerate, money grubbing, big-boobed broads pathetically latching onto the degenerate loaded ass gamblers and their loaded ass wallets.

There are also lots of dangly horse dongs.

You can learn a lot about life at a racetrack.

We stayed for a solid part of the day. We ate, we soaked in the relatively decent weather, and my mother placed a lot of two-dollar bets for us. Believe it or not, I ended up winning a fair amount of money.

The experience paid off when I returned to the racetrack on my twenty-first birthday, won more money than Bill Gates and the Hilton family combined, then moved to Tahiti and lived off a steady diet of Mojitos and island girl crotch.

Okay, so that last part never happened. It would have been pretty sweet if it had, though. Island girl crotch is a very low calorie meal. I would have slimmed down in no time at all.

On the ride home from the racetrack, my stupid little head was overflowing with stupid little ideas. I was like a collection glass at a

Bukakke party; I was frothy and overflowing, and filled to the brim with squirming, microscopic possibility.

That was gross. I never should have typed it.

The minute we got home I set forth to turn my squiggly ideas into reality. My brother and I dug through my mother's cabinets and retrieved a stack of paper cups. We rummaged through the hallway closet and found a rather large floor fan. We searched through the junk drawer in the kitchen and got our hands on some sharpie markers and a pair of scissors.

1. Paper Cups
2. Fan
3. Markers and scissors

I bet you have absolutely no idea what the hell we did with any of this garbage, do you? You're scratching you're head, right? Maybe you're even scratching your genitals?

Well, that'll teach you to find your lovin' on a city street corner, won't it? *Yep, it sure will, crabby-crotch.*

After a solid thirty minutes of work with the scissors, and the cups and the markers, we were finished. I rushed into my mother's bedroom to inform her of the situation. "Hey, Ma."

"What is it?"

I handed her a hand-made racing form and snatched her by the wrist. "Come into the kitchen."

She looked at the wonderful piece of nonsense in her hand for a moment before turning her attention again to me. She was confused. She was more confused than the time she caught me masturbating to the overly lavish Miss Piggy musical scene from the beginning of *The Great Muppet Caper*.

Don't judge me.

Moments later, she reluctantly found herself in the kitchen with her sons. There were a bunch of paper cups lined up on the table. Cut out of the top of each was something vaguely resembling a horse head.

Well, it was sort of a horse head. It could easily have been mistaken for the mushroom-shaped tip of a penis. This admittedly made the entire situation a heck of a lot weirder.

Written on each cup was a made up horse name that directly corresponded to the names on the racing form in her hand.

My little brother said exactly what I instructed him to say. "Place your bets, Mom."

Suddenly it dawned on her that her sons might be incapable of giving her grandchildren.

She made us, though. Like it or not, we belonged to her. We shot from her crotch like a couple of ooey-gooey sea to surface torpedoes. She was there when it happened, and it was way too late to take it back.

After a brief, undoubtedly sad reflection on the pair of losers she'd produced, she placed a bet.

I lifted the fan off of the floor and placed it on the kitchen table, directly behind the horse cups. Once it was in place my brother made a gun shot noise and I immediately clicked the fan on high.

The plan was for the breeze created by the fan to slide the cups from one end of the table to the other, and the first one to reach the finish line would win.

It didn't quite work out that way.

Instead they blew in every direction at once. Some of the horse cups leapt to the side and went flying off the table. A couple of them flipped over before spinning around in circles. A few others flew backward, over the fan and onto the floor. One of them even got stuck on the crappy chandelier hanging above the table.

These horses were either being ridden by jockeys that were well over the legal limit or kids with big foreheads and even bigger smiles who attend "special" classes during the day.

Luckily a couple of our crappy cup horses actually managed to go from one end of the table to the other, and one of them even crossed the finish line. What was the name of the winning horse?

You're gonna love this...

"Ladies Man."

Now that's funny.

Stupid, sarcastic Dixie cups.

THE PHONEY BOYZ

THE PHONEY BOYZ

After my parents divorced and I moved out of my father's house, my younger brother and I rarely saw each other. We would get to spend the weekends together, but that was about it. Surprisingly, we grew quite a bit closer because of the distance.

When we did get together, my little bro and I would usually spend the time making movies, or writing scripts, or planning on making movies and talking about writing scripts. We were pretty boring.

Actually, if I'm being completely honest, we did a lot more planning and talking than we did actually making anything. We were idea men. Yeah, that's it: idea men. It's not that we were actually a couple lazy sacks of donkey plop. *No. That wasn't it at all. That couldn't be it. Never. No. I swear. Don't be silly. No donkey plop.*

Around this time, the whole *prank phone call* thing was the rage. Bart Simpson had just crashed onto the scene, and a couple of middle-aged losers calling themselves *The Jerky Boys* were releasing prank call albums and making serious bank doing it. Any teenager worth his weight in Oxy-10 was fan of these guys, and my brother and I were no exception.

Which didn't make us a couple of sacks of donkey plop. Not at all. Honest. I swear.

One day, while we were sitting around and planning on writing a script, I turned to my brother and said, "You know what C, I've got an idea."

I liked to call my brother C. I still do. And I'm still not donkey plop.

Less than forty minutes later we were well on our way to becoming our very own version of The Jerky Boys, only less funny. Keep in mind that The Jerky Boys weren't that funny to begin with, so you can imagine how badly we sucked.

We came up with a pretty creative setup to make the whole thing work. We taped a microphone to the phone receiver and the microphone was connected to a mini tape recorder. We'd place a call, click record, yak it up with whoever answered, and it worked like a charm. It was simple, it was effective, and most importantly it was cheap as donkey plop. That last bit was extra important since neither of us had any money.

I'm still a bit astounded that we managed to put it all together, especially since we were basically walking, talking piles of horse plop. *Not donkey plop though.*

So what kind of prank calls did we make? Mostly the stupid kind.

I had my brother call a Christian book publisher and try to get them interested in a book about backflips .

I thought it was hilarious at the time.

I told him to say the book would be about all the great men in history who secretly enjoyed the fine art of backflipping . You know, guys like Abraham Lincoln, J. Edgar Hoover, the skinny white guy with the curly blond mop from The Greatest American Hero, and of course the legendary Dom Deluise.

I called a saddlemaker and started complaining that the saddle they sold me had rubbed my ass sore. Of course, my complaint consisted mostly of nonsensical grunts and moans. "Argh! Saddle! Agh!" I don't think I actually managed to complete a sentence.

My brother called a K-mart (the very same one that I would later end up working at) and asked the person at the service desk if he could come into the store and do some somersaults and other various tumbling maneuvers. They called him a pile of donkey plop and hung up on him.

Okay, I lied about the donkey plop thing.

I rang the local Home Depot and asked for the "wood department." They put someone on the phone and I proceeded to tell the guy that I was building a small house in my backyard for my wife. I said it needed to be exceptionally strong because she was a very large, very mean spirited bitch, who would "break it long before it broke her."

The reaction from everyone we called was pretty much the same: confusion. Truthfully, our jokes were so bad that I'm not sure they ever actually figured out if they were being pranked at all.

Our best call was one that I placed to a local clown.

"Hello?"

"Yes, is this the clown?"

"Um. Yeah, this is the clown. What can I do for you?"

"My kid has a birthday coming up and I was wondering if you were available?"

"Yeah. Sure. No problem. What day are you looking at?"

"Um. I'm not exactly sure what date my wife has planned. Um. Hold on one second. Let me double check."

"Okay. Sure."

It's at this point that my younger brother, who was on the other phone upstairs, did his best impression of a little kid and whispered, "C-c-clown?"

"What? Yes? Hello? Who's this?"

"Clo-c-c-clown?"

"Yes, I'm a clown. Who is th—"

I interrupted the clown and hopped back on the phone. "Hello? What the hell? Shit? Were you talking to my kid? God damn it! Get off the phone, Timmy! Get the hell off the phone before I crack you! Were you talking to my kid, clown? Were you?"

"I–I'm not sure, what?"

"You know this was supposed to be a surprise, right? Well, guess what? You just ruined my kid's birthday, you son of a bitch! I hope you're happy! Thanks a lot! Thanks a million!"

"Look, I didn't sa—"

"Yeah, yeah, yeah. Whatever, you jerk! You've certainly got a set on you, don't you? Where in the hell do you get off talking to my kid about anything at all, you bastard? I'm minutes away from coming over there and beating the pis—"

The clown hung up.

Okay, so maybe it wasn't hilarious. I'll admit that. Maybe it wasn't even funny. We were laughing our butts off, though.

I even scribbled up some neat-o artwork for our cassette of prank calls and dubbed us, *The Phoney Boyz*. I thought it was witty.

Plus the "Z" at the end made us seem a little less like piles of donkey plop.

PARLAN NELLISON

PARLAN NELLISON

I was at my very first comic book convention, I was twelve-years-old and I was nervous as hell.

The place was bigger than I expected it to be, filled with chubby, greasy-skinned nerds and even chubbier, greasier-skinned nerds in costumes that made them look silly, chubby and, strangely, even more greasy-skinned.

I pulled the stack of drawings under my arms closer to my body and breathed deeply. My feet wouldn't move. My legs felt heavy and my lips were dry. Even the multitudes of Spider-Man paraphernalia wasn't making me comfortable, and Spider-Man had always made me comfortable.

Why did I bring the stupid drawings? I shouldn't have brought the drawings. I might have been able to enjoy the nerd fiesta if I hadn't brought the drawings.

When my mother offered up a trip to the convention a month prior, I was excited. I was really excited. I loved comic books. I'd always loved comic books, and I was always going to love comic books. When she suggested that I bring along my drawings to show around, my excitement petered, wrinkled and crawled up into me like a chilly penis.

I didn't want to show anyone my stupid little drawings. That didn't sound fun at all. It's not that I wasn't any good, because I was pretty good – *for a twelve-year-old.*

There were going to be adults there, people older and more talented than me, people looking for jobs and struggling to feed their families. Editors and business people and such didn't have time to deal with a twelve-year-old wiener with a stack of mostly crappy *Spawn* sketches.

It was silly and I was going to feel silly doing it. *I shouldn't have brought the stupid drawings.*

My mother mashed her hand into the small of my back and pointed toward the opposite side of the room. "Why don't you go wait in that line over there?"

Fifty or so feet away, a line of Silent Bob-looking nerds was slowly forming. At the front of the line there was a small table with an elderly couple seated behind it — elderly from the perspective of a twelve-year-old, anyway.

When I didn't move, my mother nudged me again. "Go on, Steven."

I lowered my stance, shifted my weight and refused to budge. "Mom, I don't want to. I don't even know who those people are."

It was the truth. I'd never seen either of the white-haired old goats before.

"That doesn't matter, Steven." My mother squinted her eyes, looked past the line of unshaven, arty nerds, and tried to read the sign taped to the front of the table. "Look, his name is right there: Parlan." The conga line of dorks was obscuring most the letters and she was adding replacements on her own. "Parlan Nellison."

Parlan Nellison? I shook my head. "What? I don't even think that's a name."

My mother was rapidly becoming annoyed. She wedged both hands in my back, leaned into me and shoved me forward. "Yes it is, Steven! You have to start getting better at stuff like this! Now walk over there and get in line!"

I couldn't figure out why she was making me do something I clearly had no interest in doing. If she wanted to talk to old man Parlan so badly, why didn't she do it? I didn't want to talk to the guy, and I sure as hell didn't want to awkwardly offer to show him my drawings!

I wanted to call my mother a four-letter word! I wanted to kick her in the shin, tear my clothes off and run into the city screaming! I wanted to chop off her shove-happy hands and drawn my next round of Spawn drawings in the blood spurting from the stumps! I wan—

The look on her face told me that I needed to start walking.

I started walking.

I stood in that line for nearly thirty minutes, struggling to control my breathing and wiping massive amounts of sweat from my forehead. One by one the nerds plopped their oversized nerd butts beside Grandpa Parlan, opened their portfolios and began to explain the ins and outs of their work. The line was getting shorter and shorter. My neck felt itchy. My legs had transformed from concrete to loose spaghetti. I looked over at my mother. She was flashing me the *thumbs up*.

I was totally going to paint something in her blood.

The longhaired goober in front of me sat down and opened his portfolio. Suddenly I was next. As old man Parlan thumbed through the pages I was finally able to read the name on the paper hanging from the front of the table. Parlan's name wasn't even Parlan; it was Harlan.

Harlan Ellison.

At twelve-years-old, I didn't have any idea who in the hell Harlan Ellison was. I had no idea that he was one of the most influential science fiction writers of his generation. I'd never really seen *Star Trek*, and I had no idea what *The City on the Edge of Forever* was. I hadn't read *I Have No Mouth, and I Must Scream,* or *A Boy and His Dog,* and I certainly didn't know anything about him being the literary world's most famous curmudgeonly asshole.

If I had, I would've reconsidered kicking my mom in the shin.

Harlan flipped close the portfolio in front of him, shook his head, sighed deeply and waved away Mr. Nerdy McTrenchcoat. When he finally looked at me, he grimaced.

The feeling was mutual.

I didn't want to be there any more than he wanted me to be there. His old-timey arm raised and his mummified finger pointed squarely in my direction. His lips curled into an annoyed snarl and he flashed his pearly white dentures. He was moments from telling me to go play in traffic when his wife snatched his wrist, and returned his wrinkly appendage to the table.

She smiled sweetly in my direction and patted the table gently with her free hand. "Hi there."

Women.

It would have been better for all involved if she'd just let the cranky old bastard scream at me, clonk his cup of coffee off my forehead and send me on my way. Instead she had to be nice, and she had to be cordial, and she had to keep him from getting arrested for assaulting a twelve-year-old.

Women.

For the next ten minutes, Harlan begrudgingly flipped through the pages of my raggedy sketchbook and rolled his eyes while his wife remarked on just how *talented* I was. When he came to my poorly proportioned renderings of large-breasted women, he chuckled. When he came to my Liefeld-esque Youngblood drawings he moaned. When he came to the comic book I'd drawn on typing paper and stapled down the side, he nearly slammed his head against the table.

Clearly annoyed, the cranky old sack leaned back in his chair, tossed his hands into the air, and sighed a sigh so deep it made the old Jim Carey talking butt cheek gag seem subtle.

His wife tossed another *talented* my way to cover it up.

Suddenly I wanted to kick him in the shin as well. Her too. Just because.

After all the pages had been turned, the old bastard flipped my sketchbook shut and nudged me in the shoulder, clearly indicating that he wanted me to get lost. His wife shook my hand.

He did not.

I looked Harlan straight in the eye and said, "Thank you, Mr. Nellison." At that point I knew his name. I was just being a jerk.

He sort of deserved it.

When it over I shuffled through the crowd and returned to my mother's side. Believe it or not, the ditzy broad actually had the nerve to try and give me a high five.

To this day she has no idea how very close she was to getting her arms chopped off and how very close I was to crafting my next typing paper comic book with her blood.

SCHOOL SPIRIT

SCHOOL SPIRIT

I hated high school, and it hated me. The boys spent half of the day thinking of ways to kick my ass, and the other half actually kicking it. The girls looked at me like I was walking around with two fistfuls of dog poop glued to the sides of my head like earmuffs and wearing a winter jacket made of carefully patched together cow plop.

You can call me crazy if you like, but it's kind of difficult to get excited about quadratic equations when you're anticipating the *oh so wonderful* feeling of Johnny Jockstrap's foot colliding with your kidneys at 3:45 next to the dumpster out back.

"Look, mom! I'm pissing blood! I need to get to work on a paper about Operation Barbarossa and how it was the turning point of World War II, though. Guess I'll have to clean up those pesky blood splatters later!"

Don't misunderstand me; despite the occasional group dumpster beating, my high school wasn't what anyone with half a brain in their head would consider "tough."

Of course, we did have to wear ID cards around our necks. There were also random locker checks throughout the year, and metal detectors at the main entrance. Graffiti peppered the stairwells, and there was a special office on the fourth floor where a local cop was posted—but still, to the best of my knowledge no one ever went on a shooting spree or anything, at least, not while I was there.

Like most schools, every year there was a homecoming pep rally; you know, so everyone could support the team and show school spirit. *Rah, Rah, Sis Boom Bah and all that nonsense.*

On the day of the rally, the entire student body was herded into the gymnasium. Once the cattle were packed in, the principal would go into the standard speech about how the kids at his school were faster, stronger, angrier and had thicker penises than the kids from the next town over.

The football team instantly became the recipients of thunderous applause and come hither glances from those in the audience with vaginas. The cheerleaders spun and jumped, and offered up ever so brief glimpses of teenage camel toe crammed into their tiny blue underpants. A beach ball was passed around. There were signs and streamers. A few of the more dedicated decided to lather themselves in body paint.

It was loads of fun for all involved, right? *Wrong.*

As far as I was concerned, that nonsense could *eat my nuts*. It could eat my nuts then, and it can eat them now. *Hell, I'll lather them up in sauce if it'll make them go down smoother. I'll marinade them for a solid twenty-four hours before tossing them on the grill. Yeah, you heard me. I said marinade. I don't even care if that doesn't make any sense.*

Making sense can eat my nuts as well. I'll put them on a bun.

I wanted the girls to ram the beach balls right up their backsides, and the boys to roll the streamers into a fine point and slide them up their pee holes.

Sophomore year I came to a major decision: I was going to buck the trend. *I was going to play by my own rules and I was going to ditch the pep rally.*

Under normal circumstances at a normal high school, this might not have been such a difficult thing, but at my school the pep rally was mandatory. In fact, security people were posted at the exits in order to catch mad anarchist black sheep like myself, and return them safely to their pens.

I was going to have to play it smart and play it cool. For one day in my life I needed to be less Steven Novak and more Steve McQueen.

***

My eighth period ended and the teacher told us to line up and follow her to the gym for the pep rally. I made sure I was at the back of the line. Down the stairwell and to the first floor we went. We made a left at the cafeteria and headed toward the gym. When we passed by a bathroom, I quickly slipped through the door. From there it was into a stall where I dropped the toilet seat, hopped on top and quietly chuckled to myself at the sheer *genius* of my plan.

What's that?

You're saying to yourself, "This isn't very cool. Hiding on a toilet seat doesn't sound a hell of a lot like Steve McQueen."

Well, here's a bit of movie trivia for you, smartass. Apparently you haven't seen the special hush-hush directors cut of Bullitt, because Steve does exactly that. *It's there.* Trust me on this one. You don't need to go confirming it or anything. I just schooled you and you know it! *Take it like a man.*

After ten minutes I figured it was safe to make my move. I hopped off the toilet, cracked open the bathroom door and peeked out. The coast was clear.

Tiptoeing out of the bathroom, I began carefully making my way to the exit on the other side of the school. It was my thinking that the furthest exit from the actual rally was the one least likely to be guarded.

Makes perfect sense, right?

When I passed the principal's office, I crouched to make sure the receptionist didn't see me. I used an alternate route to avoid the cafeteria. My plan was working perfectly! Everything was going exactly according to plan, and I'm not the least bit ashamed to say I was pretty proud of myself.

I was really doing it! I was really ditching school and I was pulling it off in spectacular fashion! It was awesome!

No, no, wait. It wasn't awesome – *I was awesome!*

For the very first time in my life I really was Steve McQueen!

After rounding a corner at the end of the hall, I spotted the exit twenty feet away. I'd done it. I'd pulled it off. *Screw those douchebags and their douchey school spirit! Screw all the football players who had prom dates and would undoubtedly lose their virginity fifty times over before they reached their twenties! Screw all those cheerleaders with their silky skin, luscious hair, and mouth-watering chests! Screw their perky high school-loving smiles and their annoying high-pitched laughs! Screw the principal and screw the teachers! Screw the mustached janitor who would make more money putting wood chips on puke in a year then I would ever make with my art!*

Screw them all! Screw them all ten times over with the business end of a business stick! Screw them so hard they forget their names and their address and their families, and they're doomed to forever walk the streets confused and lonely and begging for change! Screw everyone in the whole damn wo-

"Hey, you! Where do you think you're going?"

Shit.

The voice came from behind me. It belonged to the girls' gym teacher.

Double shit.

Not only did my entire plan come crashing down around me in an instant, but it came crashing down because of a beefy, butch lesbian in a pair of short shorts with a whistle around her neck.

Ten minutes later I was sitting on the bleachers in the gym while everyone cheered, and the kid behind me purposely kicked me in the spine.

To the best of my knowledge I can't recall that ever happening to Steve McQueen. Even in a hush-hush director's cut.

MY MOTHER IS A LITTLE BIT GOOFY

MY MOTHER IS A LITTLE BIT GOOFY

I love my mother. She's a caring, wonderful lady who would give you the shirt off her back - as long as it's not new, and wasn't extremely expensive. Sometimes though, the woman can be a just a wee bit goofy. When I say goofy, I certainly don't mean it in a mean way. More "she's goofy" in the same way Leslie Neilsen was goofy. She's goofy with an Ernest P. Worrell vibe.

Yes, I realize how incredibly lame it is for me to actually make an Ernest P. Worrell reference. It's pathetic, and I'm ashamed. There, I admitted it. Feel better? Now that you've publically shamed me, does that make you feel better, you sick bastard?

My mother was born and grew up in what were, essentially, the slums of Chicago. She claimed on many occasions to have been some sort of "tough city girl" back in the day. The problem is that she's lived the easy life for so many years that I think the "tough city girl" either went for a very long sleep, died, or got tired of shopping for rugs and drapes, moved out, and headed back to the city. These days my mother is less "tough city girl" and much more "wimpy IKEA lady."

It was "wimpy IKEA lady" who dropped a CD case on her foot one day while walking down the stairs and literally crumbled to the floor in pain.

I walked into the room, spotted her bawling on the steps and asked with genuine concern, "Mom? What happened? Are you okay?"

She was literally crying, folded up on the floor and sobbing into her hands. She looked up at me through eyes stained with runny mascara. "Y-yes. I ju—I just—the…CD. The CD. It hit…my…foot."

I had trouble coming up with a response. "Wait. The what did what?"

"The CD case. Steven, I…it hit…my foot. I-I…dropped it."

I couldn't help but shake my head. "Wait, let me get this straight. That tiny CD case hit you on the foot? That one right there? You dropped that one right there and it landed on your foot?"

"Yes, Steven! Oh, God! Oh, God it hurts!"

I started laughing out loud at her. I had to. *Don't pretend like you wouldn't have.*

I mean, come on. Seriously? It was a measly little CD case. "Tough city girl" would have called that case a son of a bitch and stomped it to pieces. All "Wimpy IKEA lady" seemed capable of doing was sobbing uncontrollably. She needed my help to make it the rest of the way down the stairs.

I'm not kidding.

My mother also has a real issue forgetting things. She can take two entirely unrelated things and somehow mix them into a single nonsensical hodgepodge. She would then spit this newly created bastardization out of her mouth like it made perfect sense to her.

I sometimes imagine that my mother's brain looks like a massive, dangerously unorganized circus. I can picture jugglers that suck at juggling, yet happen to be juggling working chainsaws. There might even be a high-wire walker about to fall into a net with a hole in it. Or maybe there's a lion trainer that couldn't control the beast and was getting his leg chewed off. Maybe there is a pair of escaped elephants plowing over cotton candy stands and crushing the skulls of small children like ripe watermelon. It's most likely a world where the bearded lady is actually the strong man and the smallest man in the world just happens to be the bearded lady. While this of course makes no sense whatsoever, it's undoubtedly a perfect representation of my mother's brain.

One time, my brother, my mother and I decided to go to the theater to see the movie *Donnie Brasco*. On the drive over we repeated the title to my mother over and over and over again. We had to. We'd lived with her for a very long time and we knew exactly what would happen when we reached the ticket booth if we didn't.

I tried to give her an out. "Why don't you just let me get the tickets, Mom?"

"I can do it, Steven. I'm perfectly capable of ordering tickets to a movie."

"All right. Whatever you say. Donnie Brasco. Donnie Brasco. Donnie Brasco."

"I get it already, Steven. Enough."

"All right, mom. Donnie Brasco."

We arrived at the theater and made our way up to the ticket window. All she had to do was ask for three tickets to *Donnie Brasco*. It was that simple. A chimp could have pulled it off: a dumb chimp, a chimp that does a lot more throwing of feces than sign language. We went over it fifty times with her for just this reason. We couldn't have beat it into her brain any more. She was as ready as she would ever be.

"Can I help you, ma'am?"

"Yes. Um. I'd like three tickets…three for…Johnny Depke?"

Johnny what? Did she say Johnny Depke?

The guy behind the ticket window just stared at her like she'd just participated in the triple jump at last year's Special Olympics. He wasn't really mad quite so much as he was confused. He clearly felt sorry for her.

"Three for Donnie Brasco." My brother chimed in and saved her.

For my personal taste, he was a little quick on the draw. I was going to let her look like an idiot for a while longer. *Johnny Depke?* That's not even close. It's basically gibberish and it's just a step up from a barely audible grunt. Even if I grabbed a handful of marbles, stuffed them into my mouth and lit myself on fire, I bet you could have produced something that sounded more like *Donnie Brasco* than *Johnny Depke. Anyone could.*

My brother called me just the other day and we were talking specifically about the writing of this book. He asked how far along I was, and how far along I was with publishing it, and if I needed any help with the editing, that kind of stuff.

Somehow the topic of my mother worked its way into the conversation and I asked him, "Do you think she'll even read it? I'll bet you fifty bucks that she doesn't even read it."

"I'm not taking that bet."

"Why not?"

"Of course she's not going to read it. That's not even a bet."

Despite the fact that my mother claims to have never finished an entire book in her life, I thought she might make an exception in this case, but I'm thinking he was right.

Maybe if the first ten pages were nothing but ads for IKEA shelving? *Note to self: Locate contact information for Bjorn Ikea.*

HEAVENLY BOOBS AND A CAN OF SODA

HEAVENLY BOOBS AND A CAN OF SODA

Damn it. I really hated high school. I hated it so much. I hated it more than I hate Chelsea Handler, and I really, really hate Chelsea Handler.

In fact, whenever someone tells me they loved high school and that it was "the best years of their lives," I find myself immediately overcome with the desire to tie them up with razor wire, toss them in the trunk of my car, and dump the whole bloody shebang in the river.

I might not go to prison. If Casey Anthony can walk, pretty much anyone can, right? At my trial I'd just blame the whole thing on the postpartum depression card. Maybe get some lesbians to rally behind me? The only issue I can see is that I don't have a womb and haven't birthed any babies.

It doesn't hurt to try though.

Calling me a nerd in high school is a massive understatement. The word *nerd* simply doesn't cover enough ground. It's like calling Chelsea Handler *untalented*.

Actually, I didn't even fit in among the nerds. The geeks didn't want anything to do with me. The spazz kids would sooner have hung out with the JV football team, and vice-versa. Hell, even the special day kids with their towering foreheads and dribble soaked chins would scream in a manner not too dissimilar to the pod version of Donald Sutherland in *Invasion of the Body Snatchers* when they saw me coming their way.

When human beings with an IQ in single digits want nothing to do with you, well, let's just say that growing up I made a point to learn how to tie a noose out of my Star Trek Enterprise bed sheets.

Fully aware that anyone and everyone with a heartbeat and a pulse wished I had neither, I did my best to keep my distance from my peers. I kept my head down. I'd take the longer, less trafficked routes to and from class. A month into my freshman year I even stopped taking the bus home from school. This especially sucked because my house was a good three to four miles away. I needed the exercise, though. *You know, pudgy and all.*

This means that when I'm seventy I can say things to my punk-ass grandkids like, "Back in my day, I had to walk three miles home in the snow" and not be lying or in need of my pills.

Despite the distance, walking home proved to be exactly the change of pace I was looking for. I was getting exercise. It was quiet, maybe even a little relaxing. It didn't hurt that in one of the houses I passed lived a dark-skinned, dark-haired MILF who would spend her afternoons tanning on her front lawn in a barely-there bikini, which showed off a rack sent down from a Hooters restaurant somewhere in Heaven itself. That was pretty nice.

Yep, I had exercise, clean air, mostly decent weather and an ample set of boobs on display three out of five days of the week. Everything was coming up Steve.

That is, until I got hit in the back of the head with a McDonalds bag.

A damn McDonalds bag. This mostly disgusting bag of grease was launched at me by a group of jackasses from school in a passing car. A slimy paper bag filled with the sort of stuff nightmares are made of, whacking you on the back of the head at 30mph, can ruin a perfectly nice day like you wouldn't imagine. It's worse than some poor Make a Wish that wanted so very badly to meet a television star before he passed into the great beyond, and instead got sent Rosie O'Donnell.

When you take into consideration the fact that stuff like this was happening to me all the time back then, I'd grown an uncanny ability to simply let it pass and go on with my life. My outer shell was harder than my penis. I couldn't be hurt, not by anything or anyone.

I wiped the smeared burger grease from my cheek and continued on, until the same thing happened two days later, and the Monday after that and once more on Tuesday. Then Thursday and the Tuesday following that.

I had so much processed meat in my hair I was beginning to look like Mayor McCheese.

Hoping to avoid any further drive-by pelting, I began taking different routes home. This worked for a while, but somehow those assholes and their grease-laden arteries managed to find me. I tried ducking behind trees and fences and crouching behind cars and garbage cans. I would bolt from one hiding place to the next like a soldier dodging incoming sniper fire. McDonalds, Burger King, random disgusting food collected from the cafeteria, at one point or another I've been hit with it all. There was once even a homemade tuna sandwich still in its little plastic bag. If it was eatable, it whipped in my general direction at a high rate of speed.

One day a completely full can of Pepsi clonked me in the shoulder, flipped and twisted in the air before slamming against the concrete sidewalk and exploding. Soda began spurting in every direction. It soaked my pants. In a manner of seconds I was sticky and dripping and covered with sugary-fizz.

Guess who was watching me from the comfort of her front lawn?

Yep, heavenly boobs.

The sound of aluminum smacking bone and the subsequent spraying must have scared her because she was on her feet, staring at me with wide eyes and breathing heavily. Every time she inhaled the oversized orbs on her chest would bounce and sway and jiggle so very beautifully in their minuscule holders. The expression on her face — which I'm rather astounded I noticed with all the jiggling — was one of both sadness and disgust. To her I was barely a human being. I was a homeless puppy missing a leg and wearing one of those big white cones around its head. As bad as she might have felt, at the same time I was infected with rabies. It was dangerous to come near me.

Let me just say this and make it perfectly clear to anyone listening in this world or the next. *If there is a God, and if I actually ever get the chance to meet him, I swear to you the first thing I'm going to do is punch him in the solarplexus. When he's keeled over, I'm giving him a wedgie. After that, I'll most likely haul my booty out of there, because once he gets his bearings I'm pretty sure he could mop the floor with me.*

Heavenly boobs noticed me staring at her orbs, snagged her towel, covered up and scurried back to her house. I watched her booty shake as she ran away. I might have been covered in sugary, caffeine loaded awfulness, but I wasn't blind.

THE MIAMI HEAT TAKE THE TITLE

THE MIAMI HEAT TAKE THE TITLE

The starting line-up was as follows:

Center: Karl Rhodes.

Power Forward: Steve "Air" Novak

Small Forward: Marcus Dupree

Shooting Guard: "Quick" Nick Novak

Point Guard: Cubby Dodger

At this point you're no doubt saying to yourself, *What in the hell is this moron babbling about? Those names have nothing to do with the Miami Heat.*

Well, you're right on both counts. I am indeed, a moron, and generally none of the names listed above are associated with the Miami Heat in any way.

Here's the thing: When my younger brother would come to visit on the weekends, he and I would almost always end up playing basketball in the driveway. We didn't just *play* basketball though. While every other *normal* kid on the block would settle into a nice game of one on one or maybe even a round of horse, the Novak Brothers were acting out entire games as members of a fictional version of the Miami Heat.

We lived in Chicago in the 90s, when The Bulls were pumping out championships faster than Stephenie Meyer pumps out terrible novels.

So, why the Heat? *I dunno. We were dumb?*

In case you missed it, our roster included a player named *Marcus Dupree*. This is apparently what two white kids from the suburbs believed a black guy was supposed to be named and this is embarrassing on any number of levels.

Here's how our bizarre little games would go down: When the Heat played, the Lakers, or the Nets, or the Celtics, or whoever, the little bro and myself would shoot for both teams. While we were shooting for both teams - on one hoop - we also took over the role of the announcers as well.

We'd call out things like, "Dodger passes to Rhodes. Rhodes shoots it outside to Nick Novak. Novak dribbles, searches for an opening, throws it inside to his brother, Air Novak with the thunder dunk!"

Keep in mind that my *thunder dunk* was really more of a layup, but then, I wasn't playing games in the Boston Garden either.

Suspend a little disbelief, jerk.

We had a rule that if we scored baskets as the opposing team and kept missing shots as our team, then it was a *too bad so sad* sort of situation and we'd have to allow the other team to *beat us*.

There were ways around that rule, though.

Somehow the other team seemed to always be shooting tough fall-away shots from half court, while our team was inside the free throw line hitting layups all night long.

Bad luck for them, huh?

Believe it or not, a time arrived when our Miami Heat team had won back-to-back-to-back NBA Championships, and even we were getting a little sick of ourselves. We needed a break. We needed to let someone else have their moment in the sun.

Here was our solution:

We'd just beaten the Boston Celtics, in Boston, and were on our way to the NBA finals for the fourth straight season. Our entire team was celebrating at center court when the Celtics coach came storming into the large group of players. He was hootin' and he was hollerin', and he was generally pissed off about the way we were showing disrespect to his team and the Boston fans.

Makes perfect sense, right?

Anyway, someone on our team pelted a basketball off his forehead.

The old timer dropped like a sack of potatoes to the parquet floor. He was out cold. He wasn't moving. The paramedics rushed to his side and the crowd noise dropped to a whisper. It was all over ESPN. The mainstream media picked up on the story and ran with it as well.

Despite the on-court drama, we went on to win the NBA title that year. Unfortunately, it was a win tainted by controversy, especially from the fans in Boston, who were screaming for our blood.

During the off-season, the Celtics coach petitioned the league to reprimand us, citing unsportsmanlike conduct. After being reviewed by the NBA — Um, *decisions* board or something, it was decided that our entire team would be forced to sit out the next season.

Which again makes perfect sense, right?

Of course it does.

Shut up.

The "basketball off the head incident," followed by the fact that our entire team spent a season at home, put an end to the Heat's plans at a Five-Peat. Yep, we lost because we weren't allowed to play.

Sweet Lord, we were lame.

Anyway, there were a lot of broken hearts in Miami that year. Children sat silently on empty basketball courts trying to make sense of a world in which a basketball bounced off a head could mean an end to a season. Women cried into the oversized official replica jerseys they wore to bed at night. They curled into the fetal position and clutched their "Quick" Nick Novak posters to their chests. Grown men drowned their sorrows in bottles of beer at the local Miami watering holes and shelf after shelf at Footlockers everywhere were stacked to the brim with unsold pairs of "Air" Novak sneakers.

These were dark days, my friends: dark days indeed.

The year after our suspension the Heat returned stronger than ever. We ended up winning the NBA Championship for a fifth time, much to the dismay of the Celtics coach.

My brother and I were idiots.

My brother and I are still idiots.

DEAR MR. HUNTINGTON, I AINT' LEARNED SHIT

DEAR MR. HUNTINGTON, I AINT' LEARNED SHIT

I think my mother thought I was an idiot. *In fact, I'm pretty sure of it.*

I was a terrible student in high school. I was failing pretty much everything except art, including gym, and despite my mother's constant attempts to set me on the straight and narrow, when it came to my schoolwork, things didn't seem to be improving.

The problem wasn't that I was dumb. The problem was that I didn't give a shit. I didn't care how bad my grades were, or how much worse they would eventually get. It didn't bother me one bit that my mother thought I was a lazy doofus, and my teachers cringed every time they saw me in the hall. It didn't matter that the letter "F" had become synonymous with my name, and it unfortunately had nothing to do with how much I was getting laid because the ladies weren't into me and I wasn't getting laid—unless you count the magic marker face I drew on my hand as a "lady."

If that's the case, I got laid a lot.

I also couldn't have cared less about college, or my future, or any of the things people who eventually find success in life and have more than sixteen dollars in the bank and some old comic books in their closets think about. I honestly just wanted to be left alone. I wanted to silently brood in my bedroom with my Nine Inch Nails albums, the stack of porn hidden under my bed, and my mostly predictable teenage angst.

Unfortunately, my mother wasn't a Nine Inch Nails fan.

"Steven, I signed you up for some tutoring sessions at the Huntington Learning Center."

Gulp.

In case you hadn't figured it out already, that was her, my mom. You see, she didn't want me living in her house and still slogging around in my Spider-Man boxers well into my thirties. She wasn't quite as ready as I was to give up on my grades and/or my future.

Jerk.

If you've never heard of The Huntington Learning Center, let take a moment to explain what it is. Basically the fine people at Huntington are overly expensive tutors. They probably have degrees and they probably know what they're doing for the most part. Their various degrees undoubtedly state that very fact.

Too bad their degrees didn't mean shit to me. Their degrees might as well have been scribbled on soiled toilet paper as far as I was concerned. I didn't want to learn. Unless they were teaching me fifteen dollars (which doesn't make any sense) for the newly released Nirvana's Greatest Hits album, or how to get the football team to stop kicking my ass next to the dumpster in the school parking lot, I didn't have any interest in learning. Learning was stupid. It was annoying too. I had Marilyn Manson lyrics to angrily listen to and marker-lady fists to screw. *Learning could kiss my ass.*

I considered telling my mother that I wouldn't go, but she tossed her "your dumb ass is going no matter what" look my way. *There was no getting out of it.*

Keep in mind that I was a freshman in high school at the time. I didn't have a car, or the prospect of a car, or a bike, or even a decent public transportation system, or legs long enough to carry the weight of my pudgy torso more than fifty feet before collapsing.

Since Huntington was in the next town over, I had to order myself a short bus to drive me there, drop me off and pick me up twice a week. I'd get home from school, call myself a bus and arrive at Huntington a mere forty-five minutes later.

It wasn't all bad though.

"Hi, Steven! How's everything going today?"

That was my main tutor-lady. She was young-ish, and she was overly perky (I'm not referring to her personality), and she was always wearing low cut blouses.

See? There's always a silver lining.

As much as I appreciated her attire, I actually sort of hated the fact that she was assigned to me. I wanted someone old, maybe someone with four or five big-ass warts on her face, and glasses, and boobs so droopy she could tuck them into her bloomers. I wanted someone who might have gone for an orgasm ride on Lincoln's beard.

Embarrassed, I mumbled something vaguely resembling the word "fine."

I bothered me that my Huntington lady thought I was a dummy. Not that I ever had a chance of getting into her tutor-britches or anything. And it certainly didn't bother me enough to buckle down and focus on my studies to impress her. *It still bothered me, though.*

Math was first on the agenda during my visits. My *boober* – or, um, I mean *tutor*, would get out her little workbook, spend fifteen or twenty minutes going over some problems with me, and eventually slide a test in my direction.

At least, I think that's what happened. My eyeballs were busy rolling around in the heft of her cleavage like a pig in shit the entire time. *It's possible I'm not remembering things exactly right.*

After I inevitably bombed the test, we'd discuss what I did wrong and when that was over I'd grab my climbing gear and descend the curvature of her *oh so creamy* left breast like a beard-toting Swiss climber scaling the alps. *Actually no. That's a lie.*

Truthfully, we just moved onto writing. The writing section of my Huntington adventure was basically more of the same. BouncyTutor McJiggleChest would get out a workbook, we'd go over some stuff, and she'd leave me to take a test. In this case, however, the term "take a test" actually meant "watch her hips sway as she walked away and drool dripped from my lips."

If you're thinking that I sound like the world's biggest pervert, lay off. I was barely fifteen at the time. Like most fifteen-year-old boys, I had been cursed with an erection that wouldn't die. There wasn't any blood going to my brain. The blood had bought a condo on the beach down south. It adopted a dog from the local pound and it made some friends, and it had already changed the billing address on its credit cards. It wasn't going anywhere. *At least not until I hit my thirties.*

ButterCheeks McNippleShirt returned fifteen minutes later. "Okey dokey, let's have a look, shall we?" She bounced when she sat down. My heart fluttered.

Did I say heart? *I meant wiener.*

As she started to scan my answers she shook her head, sighed a sigh of absolute defeat and began making checkmarks. Halfway through, she stopped. The hypnotic ripples in her chest meat disappeared. Her head lifted. Her jaw locked and her eyes narrowed. She bared her teeth and coiled her fingers into a fist. "Really?"

She looked pissed. I'd never seen her look pissed before, but she looked pissed.

I wasn't sure why. "What?"

MassiveOrbs McSilkyUdders spun my answers around and slid them across the table with a frustrated growl. At first, I didn't notice anything wrong. Everything looked normal. My answers were brief, and they were wrong, and she had put a checkmark by every one of them.

Then I got to question eight. My answer to question eight was "Boobs."

Damn it.

My answer to question nine was "Tits."

Double damn it.

My answer to question ten was "Nips."

Fuck my life.

I didn't even know I was writing it. I swear I didn't! It was my penis blood! *It was that damn penis blood I tell you!* My penis blood had hopped in a Winnebago and taken a surprise vacation north to visit some family, where it threw a party, got everyone drunk and trashed my brain.

AngryTutor McPissedOff called my mother and sent me home. It was decided by both parties that maybe The Huntington Learning Center wasn't exactly the place I needed to be.

I didn't learn a damn thing during my brief stint at Mr. Huntington's House of Plentiful Knockers and Tiny Shirts, unless you count the new masturbation fodder. *You probably don't, though.*

-Steven Novak-

I'M SUPPOSED TO BE A LOGGER

I'M SUPPOSED TO BE A LOGGER

"Can we ride again?"

"No, sorry. You'll have to get back in line."

"But there's only like fifteen people in line! Come on, big guy. Let us go one more time. Be a pal. What's it gonna hurt?"

"I'm, sorry. You'll have to get back in line."

"You know what? Fuck it. Fuck you too! This is so fucking stupid! There's no one in line and you're gonna make us get out and walk all the way around in order to ride again? Are you fucking nuts? Gimme a break!"

"I'm sorry, sir."

"No you're not. If you were sorry you'd just let us stay in the goddamn boat! This is so stupid! It's fucking insane! Come on kids, the asshole is going to make us get off and walk all the way around to get back on."

"I'm sorry I've set a bad example for your children."

"Excuse me?"

That was the sort of nonsense I had to deal with on a daily basis while gainfully employed as a ride operator at Six Flags Great America in Gurnee, Illinois.

The ride I was assigned to was called *The Logger's Run*. It was a water ride. Employees were required to call it by its technical name, however: *The Flumes*. I'm still not entirely sure what the word *flumes* means, or where it comes from originally, and honestly I don't even care enough to take thirty seconds and Google it. I can't think of one single instance in which I've had use for it outside of my time at Great America, anyway.

Not once. Not ever.

Maybe it would work in a foreplay situation? You know, something like: "Baby I'm gonna do you good with this here flume of mine."

No? Yeah, probably not. Flume *isn't a very sexy word. The word* dong *is sexier, and* dong *isn't very sexy at all.*

Anyway, every morning I was expected to arrive at Six Flags at least forty-five (unpaid) minutes early. I needed the extra time to make my way "backstage," get to my locker, order up a fresh costume, get dressed and make my way to the opposite side of the park where my ride was.

The costume in question, for those of us *lucky* enough to be stationed on *The Loggers Run*, was basically a pair of jeans so crazily tight that they not only made even the simplest movements impossible, but also put the baby elephant trunk and marbles on display for anyone sneaking a glance. I also had to slide into a brown shirt made of an odd felty (which isn't a word) material, with an oversized collar and a neckline that plunged so deep it exposed far more of my doughy, sporadically-haired chest area than anyone wanted exposed.

Don't get me wrong, the shirt looked bonkers great on the female employees – so great it made wearing those tight jeans all the more difficult. It might have even worked on a muscular dude. *I don't make judgments.*

Putting my man boobs on display was a terrible idea, though. It's always been a terrible idea and it'll always be a terrible idea. My moobs are like religious cults and the Kardashians.

The thing about working at Great America (and I imagine this is the same at all theme parks) is that people in the park have paid large sums of money for their tickets, and because of that they seem to think they own the damn place.

Dropping fifty bucks doesn't make you a king and it sure as shit doesn't give you the right to act like an idiot. Sorry. It just doesn't. Dropping a thousand bucks doesn't give you that right. Dropping a million bucks might.

Let's test it. Someone drop me a million bucks and treat me like shit.

The question I was most commonly asked while working was, "Can we ride again?"

My answer was always, "No, I'm sorry, you'll have to get back in line."

The response to my no was usually something along the lines of, "That's a fucking stupid policy! Come on! Just let us ride again! It's not gonna hurt anything! Don't be such a little prick, you little prick fuck!"

Okay, maybe there wasn't so many "pricks" or "fucks," but you get my point.

This happened every day - for eleven hours a day – nonstop. It was nauseating.

Working at Six Flags was a marathon. It required fortitude of will and an uncanny ability to keep my emotions at bay. I was constantly fighting the urge to grab every one of the *ride again* idiots by their shirt collars and scream in their faces, "I make seven dollars an hour! Seven measly dollars!" I pictured myself squeezing their necks until their eyes bulged and their faces began to turn as purple and blue as the tip of a penis moments before release. I imagined myself knocking them to the ground, lifting my boot, and stomping it into their groin. "I don't make decisions, you moron! I make seven dollars an hour to not make decisions! If I let you get on that boat, I get fired, and if I get fired I make zero dollars an hour!" I wanted to wrap my fingers around their necks one more time, and squeeze until my knuckles turned white. I wanted to squeeze so hard their heads exploded and their brain matter fell from the heavens like rain. *It would have been so beautiful and freeing. It would have been the end of The Shawshank Redemption brought to life in Gurnee, Illinois.*

For example, take the conversation I was having with this large 240 to 250-pound guy at the beginning of this story. The guy's boat had just pulled into the station with himself, a woman I assumed was his wife, and his two kids sitting behind. I had about ninety seconds once a boat pulled into the station to get the old riders out and the new riders in before it cycled and was shot out of the loading area. This guy was going to push that ninety seconds to the max.

"Can we ride again?"

"No, sorry. You'll have to get back in line."

"But there's only like fifteen people in line! Come on, big guy. Let us go one more time. Be a pal. What's it gonna hurt?"

"I'm, sorry. You'll have to get back in line."

"You know what? Fuck it. Fuck you too! This is so fucking stupid! There's no one in line and you're gonna make us get out and walk all the way around in order to ride again? Are you fucking nuts? Gimmie a break!"

"I'm sorry, sir."

"No you're not. If you were sorry you'd just let us stay in the goddamn boat! This is so stupid! It's fucking insane! Come on kids, the asshole is going to make us get off and walk all the way around to get back on."

"I'm sorry I've set a bad example for your children."

"Excuse me?"

I was being a smart ass. I knew I was doing it and I didn't care. The end of my rope had been reached and it was slathered in grease. I was sick of climbing. I didn't even want to hold on anymore. Maybe I should have just kept my mouth shut, but it had been a particularly long and especially annoying day. *I blame the Warner Bros. Corporation more than myself on this one.*

"What? Did you just say that I'm setting a bad example for my children? Because I haven't done anything wrong here, you're the jackass who won't let my family ride again even though there's no one in line!"

The guy's kids and wife had already gotten out of the boat. They were heading for the exit and yet this guy refused to move. He was sitting there, soaking wet, and arguing with a sixteen-year-old kid about something the kid obviously had no control over.

His wife grabbed him by the arm. "Come on Fred. Just forget about it. Let's go."

Fred shucked her away, his face redder than the rear end of a well-spanked gimp. AngryFred slammed his hand on the front of the boat. "No! Who does this little prick think he is? I'm not forgetting about anything!"

His boat was rapidly nearing the halfway point. My supervisor noticed there was a problem and decided to intervene. "Is there a problem here, sir?"

"Yes there's a fucking problem! All my family and I wanted to do was ride again and this little dickface won't let us!"

Dickface? I always thought I was more of a vagina face, myself.

"Plus he's giving me lip! This is what I paid good money for? Really?"

As Foul-MouthedFred screamed at my supervisor (who was seventeen-years- old) I noticed that his boat was nearing the *Critical Loading Point*.

Ooh. Sounds dangerous, doesn't it?

Basically, the *Critical Loading Point* was the spot at which we were no longer allowed to load *guests* on the boat because they might slip and fall, and possibly die. Or worse, they might slip and fall, and possibly sue.

StubbornFred was intent on remaining exactly where he was. He wasn't going anywhere. This was his battle for the day and damn it, he was going to win it!

He motioned for his kids to hop in the boat with him and barked, "Danny! Jessie! Get back in, we're going on again!" His wife buried her head in her hands, grabbed the little girl (who I assume was Jessie) by her wrist and headed for the exit. Though he looked terrified, Danny hopped in the boat alongside his father moments before it left the loading station.

Fred assumed he'd won. He believed he'd beaten the sixteen-year-old punk with the smart mouth, and the sixteen-year-old punk's seventeen-year-old supervisor in their disgustingly low shirts and super-tight jeans. He was proud. It was his greatest accomplishment. It was something to tell the boys at work about, and it was going to make a bonkers-fantastic story at the next barbeque. He was excited and he was happy, he was laughing his ass off. StupidFred leaned over and gave his son a pre-ride noogie. He pumped his fist and readied himself to get soaked again! He was getting his fifty bucks worth! Rules and common sense, and basic human decency had been tossed out the window and he couldn't have cared less!

This was the defining moment in Fred's life, until I hit the ride stop button and a huge steel wall popped in front of his boat.

He wasn't going anywhere.

Fred immediately turned to me. He leaned out of the boat, pointed a finger in my direction and screamed, "Fuck you! Fuck you, asshole!"

People are nuts. It's as simple as that.

-Steven Novak-

ROSE TAKES IT OFF

ROSE TAKES IT OFF

I was a virgin throughout high school. I never poked a pair of boobs. I never squeezed a buttock that wasn't my own. I never kissed a girl on the lips, or the face, or the hand, or blew one in her direction from across a room. I never went on a date. I never even had a female look at me without screaming at me to stop staring before unleashing their boyfriends on me.

I was as pure as a newborn baby, with a slightly more impressive penis. *Only slightly, though.*

In fact, the only parts of a naked woman I'd ever seen were either in my head or in any of the various pornographic materials I'd managed to catch a glimpse of over the years. To say that I was a teeny bit *hard* up for human contact would be the understatement of the century, the equivalent of saying Michael Bay is a bad director.

While true, it doesn't even come close to telling the whole story.

In my senior year in high school I earned a scholarship to an art college in Ohio. It wasn't too long afterward that I learned the required courses of the first year included a figure drawing class—a nude figure drawing class.

Oh, yeah. I was finally going to see some real life boobs!

I fully understand just how pathetic that last sentence must have read to the vast majority of you. I assure you, it sounded just as pathetic in my head. I'm not proud of it. It's not something I'm going to put on my resume or tell the grandkids when I'm old. It's out there, and I can't take it back. What's done is done.

At the time I didn't even care that there would likely be a guy or two thrown into the mix. I'd been in locker rooms. I could suffer though a few eyefuls of penis for the chance to gaze upon the flesh and blood form of a naked female.

It was going to be awesome. It was going to be naked women awesome, which is the most absolute awesome of awesome when you're a sad and lonely eighteen-year-old.

Months passed. During that time I moved to Ohio and I settled into the dorms at school. I was raring to go! I was chomping at the bit! I was chomping at the bit, raring and going with the chomp!

I don't know what that last one is supposed to mean and I really don't care.

That's how excited I was.

It was the first day of the figure-drawing class. I was at my desk with my pencils out and pad of paper opened. My fingers were tapping on the desk anxiously. They wouldn't stop. The instructor said something along the lines of, "The model is getting ready. She'll be out in a moment."

She'll? He used the word "she'll."

Hells to the yeah.

It was a woman, a girl, a female, a homosapien with sexual organs entirely different than my own. Whatever you wanted to call it, it was going to have a womb.

'Fo shizzle.

I slid my midsection a little more underneath the desk, on the off chance that something began to stir below. I wanted to be prepared. *Keepin' it real, homie!*

Moments later, the model walked into the room. She was at least seventy-five.

Dayum.

In hobbled an elderly woman named Rose. Her face was like a catcher's mitt and her hair like an old bird's nest. She was probably one of Thomas Jefferson's mistresses, and it was safe to assume she'd been getting discounts at Denny's since the 80s.

Rose dropped her robe, and my world crumbled with it. She looked like a garbage bag filled with drippy-wet pee-poo diapers. She looked like a Barbie doll someone melted in the sun. She looked like a textbook definition of the word *gravity*. Needless to say, my fears about hiding my midsection were completely unfounded. *In fact, my penis took the initiative and hid itself.*

I spent the next hour and a half drawing Rose in various positions I wished she'd never gotten into while listening to her complain that she was cold, or aching, or that she needed a rest because the arthritis in her hands was acting up.

As I stared at the wrinkly exterior she called flesh and I called the Devil's hammocks, all I could think was, *"Those aren't supposed to be down that low, are they?"*

I also never wanted to eat, or see someone eat, or be in the presence of a roast beef sandwich again.

Halfway through the class, the instructor gave everyone a break. While most of the students went outside to smoke a cigarette or throw up, or throw up then use the cigarette to burn their eyes, I sat in stunned silence. It's not that I couldn't move so much as I didn't want to move. I never wanted to move again.

With everyone gone, Rose put on her robe and started walking around the room, looking at the drawings everyone had done of her. She nodded her head at some and shook it at others. Turned *out she was a real art snob — you know, for a bag of old beef jerky.*

She eventually made her way to me and stood behind me with one hand on her hip and the other scratching at those pesky black hairs dangling from her chin. There was little more than a thin sheen of nylon separating me from her wrinkled nakedness.

She was quiet for a minute, examining my work with her discerning, cataract-riddled eyes. When she'd seen all she needed to see, Rose leaned down and pinched my cheek from behind. "That's really wonderful, sweetie." I'm not even kidding. She pinched my damn cheek.

Just like my Grandma used to do.

How I made it through the second half of class while comparing Rose to my nanny *(who by a cruel piece of fate, also happened to have been named Rose)* is completely beyond me.

Rose, the nude model, was the very first woman who ever flashed me her junk while in something fairly close to the doggie-style position.

Rose reminded me of my grandma.

Sometimes all you can do is laugh at life. Other times you want to throw a brick at it.

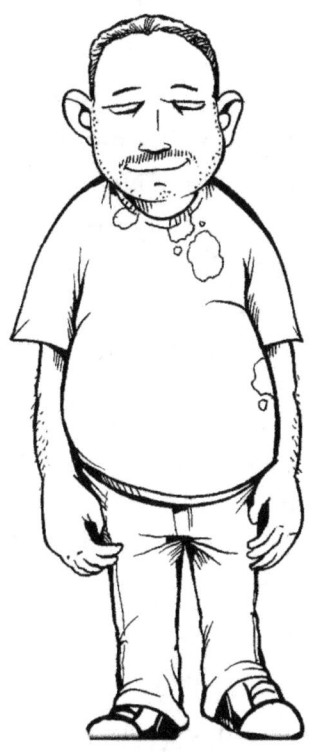

MIGUEL AND HIS MAGIC CARDS

MIGUEL AND HIS MAGIC CARDS

Freshmen year in college I was assigned three roommates. The first was Stewart. Stewart was a Christian kid from, Indiana. I think he even brought his Bible with him. Nice guy, though. The second was Rolando. Rolando was a gay guy from Puerto Rico. He didn't bring much with him, besides his thong. *Shiver.* Last but not least was Miguel. If someone were to compare my roommates to The Three Stooges, Miguel would have been Larry. *Miguel was useless.*

Like Rolando, Miguel came originally from Puerto Rico. Unlike Rolando, he wasn't gay, he wasn't over six feet tall, and he didn't weigh less than one hundred and twenty pounds. He didn't care how his hair looked, or if it was combed at all. He didn't like to shower, or bathe, or clean the parts of him in desperate need of cleaning. He was pretty good at smelling like fried plantains, though, so I guess he had that going for him.

Despite their familiar birthplace, Rolando and Miguel couldn't have been more different. Miguel was maybe five feet tall, he weighed around two hundred and fifty pounds and he really, really liked the ladies, though he had absolutely no idea how to get them.

Standing beside each other, they looked like a demented Telemundo version of Laurel and Hardy.

Wait – let me take that back. Now that I think about it, they did have one thing in common. They loved annoying the piss out of me. In fact, if there was an *"Annoying the Fuck Out of Steve Championships,"* these two would have been contenders for the title.

Donald Sutherland would have been a close third. *God damn you, Sutherland.*

In order to reinforce my point, let me take you through an average day in my life with Miguel. I'd get up early in the morning and stroll through our disgusting little kitchen area on my way to our equally disgusting bathroom so I could stand naked in our disease-infested shower. Along the way I'd almost always stumble across five to six plates of half-eaten rice and moldy glop. As much as Miguel loved to cook this stuff, he never seemed to finish it, and he never cleaned his plate. Instead he'd just leave it on the counter, or the chairs, or the floor. I even once found a plate of this garbage in the shower.

Don't ask.

I'm still not sure what it was, but it stunk like my grandmother's crotch minutes after he whipped it up and sitting out all night rarely improved the stench. By morning it smelled like *your* grandmother's crotch too: both our grandmothers, scissoring on the kitchen floor. *Good luck sleeping with that image in your brain.*

Our bathroom was always a mess. Miguel never cleaned it. When it was his turn to tidy up, he added more filth instead. There was mold in the shower. It was black, and it was slimy and slippery like seaweed. There was permanent brown ring on the brown-stained toilet. There was grime on the sink, and film on the floor, and the remnants of popped zits, still stuck to the mirror.

There was a cockroach. I called him Ted.

The filth I could deal with, though. As disgusting as it was, the filth couldn't be blamed entirely on Miguel. I could have cleaned it. If I wanted to spend my days as a butler for my insensitive roommates, I could have cleaned it. The worst thing about Miguel was his Magic: The Gathering cards.

One afternoon, I was trying to get some of that sleep I spoke of only sentences ago, but it was completely impossible with Miguel and his friends in the next room listening to music and playing with their Magic: The Gathering cards.

Look, I'm a dork. I always have been and I always will be. I know way too much about Star Trek, my closets are filled with boxes of comic books, and my social skills are nonexistent.

That being said, if you combined every dorky, loser thing I've ever said or done into one giant dork stew, it wouldn't be nearly as dorky as listening to M.C. Hammer and playing Magic: The Gathering until two in the morning. *It's not even a competition.*

Miguel and his pals did this every night, into the wee hours of the morning. They'd laugh and flip cards and munch away on plates of foul-smelling rice without a care in the world. They'd do it all while I was trying to sleep.

I spent my nights half-awake, dreaming of dragons wielding broad swords in parachute pants and claiming they were 2 *legit 2 quit.*

It was infuriating.

"Miguel, think you could turn off the music? I've got to get up early."

I was polite about it the first time. I had to live ten feet from the guy and there was no point in making enemies. Miguel pretended he was sorry. He smiled, nodded his head and lowered Hammer's hokey 90s family-friendly rap to a reasonable level.

Ten minutes later it was back to normal.

The sound of cards flapping and dorks giggling managed to worm its way into my ear and poked me in the folds of my brain. I could hear their teeth chomping and their throats swallowing. I envisioned a table full of Orcs and Elves, and various stats that made no sense whatsoever.

I crawled from bed and opened the door. "Jesus Christ, Miguel! What the hell?"

Again he offered up his most *sincere* apologies and again he lowered the volume on Hammer. His friend laid down a card and claimed he was "attacking with his Rampager Elf." I had to bite my tongue to keep from punching them all in the face.

Ten minutes later and Hammer was *hurtin' em* again.

Now I was pissed. Biting my tongue wouldn't work anymore. If I tried to bite it, I would have chomped it off. I wanted to tear Miguel's head from his shoulders, take a dump down his torso, and fill his neck hole with my piss. I wanted to chop him into pieces and send the pieces to Hammer's mansion. I wanted to rip open his stomach, tie his intestines into a rudimentary hammock, and get the sleep I deserved.

Half awake and angered beyond the point of reason, I shuffled through the dark to my desk, grabbed my boom box and my soundtrack from the movie Halloween. (Yes, I owned that.) I popped it in, turned it on and blasted the volume.

You see, I could be scary when I wanted to. I've always been a pretty big guy, and even if I wasn't a big guy, Miguel was a very little guy. I never talked, I was usually angry about something or other and I never smiled. Smiling made my face hurt. If I'd smiled, people might have opened up to me; I might have even made a couple friends.

At that point in my life I didn't want friends. I didn't want acquaintances, or business associates, or random passersby. I wanted corpses. On that particular afternoon, I wanted Miguel's corpse specifically.

Once the infamous Halloween theme was blasting loud enough for Miguel and his Magic pals to hear, I opened the door and stared at them from the shadows of my room. My chest was heaving and my jaw locked. My hands were pulled so tightly into fists that my knuckles had turned white. When I spoke, I spoke slowly. "If you don't turn that fucking shit down, right now, I swear to Jesus, the Devil, and Buddha that I am going to fucking kill each and every one of you. Do you understand?"

Miguel apologized for real. He turned off the music completely.

I stared at him just a little bit longer, not really saying anything, just breathing and grinding my teeth together and imagining how his skin would look as a vest.

His Magic buddies were more than a little disturbed. *Rampaging Elves were of no use to them anymore.* They never played Magic in our dorm room again and I was completely M.C. Hammer free for the next fifteen years.

To be fair though, so was pretty much everyone else.

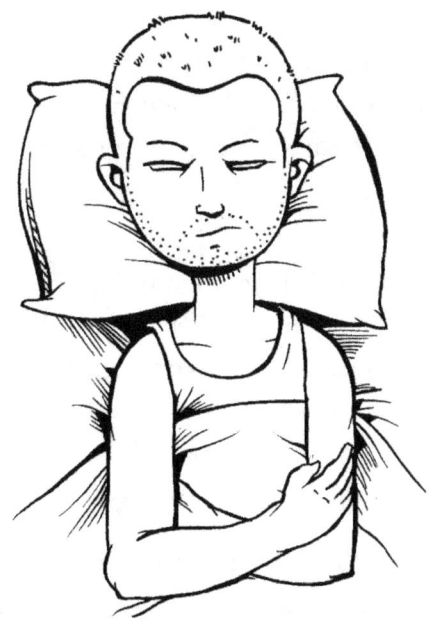

A ROOM FULL OF NAKED LADIES

A ROOM FULL OF NAKED LADIES

When I was a freshman in college I shared a dorm room with three other guys. Okay, that's not entirely true. I actually shared a bathroom and a rather pathetic kitchen area with three other guys. I only had to share the bedroom with one of them.

His name was Stewart.

Stewart was from a little town in Indiana I'd never heard of and from his description it sounded a heck of a lot like the fictional town of Mayberry. I imagined apple pies on windowsills, and cows taking dumps on front lawns, and rows of corn, and good Christian folk thumbing through their Bibles, and the occasional midnight rendezvous with the sheep in the barn. You know, the basics.

I know this is a wee bit off topic, but if you happen to be one of those creepy guys that has a shaving fetish, is getting your hands on a set of shears and going to town on a sheep the absolute sexiest thing in the world? Just wondering.

Anyway, the room that Stewart and I shared was tiny. Actually it was tinier than tiny. It was teensy tiny. The beds were built into the far wall and the only thing separating them was a wardrobe that went from ceiling to floor. As you can no doubt imagine, it sort of sucked having to sleep in such close quarters.

Making matters worse was the fact that Stewart was a loser, just like me, and being a loser, he never went anywhere. Ever. He was *always* there. He was always in the room and always no more than five to ten feet away. He was always with me, for an entire school year.

Did I stress the fact that he was *always* there? I did? Okay, just making sure.

Stewart was stuck to me like no-talent-bitchery is stuck to Paris Hilton. He was stuck to me like repetitive paranormal romance nonsense is stuck to the book industry. He was stuck to me like Pooh in the honey tree.

I was a perfectly healthy boy/man and I wasn't anywhere near getting laid, and honestly, I needed some time alone to take care of certain…*things.* The area just south of my belly button was backed up like a California highway during rush hour. I needed to release some pressure, and I'm not talking about the pressure built up in my kick ass, retro Reebok Pumps.

With Stewart ten feet away at any given point during the day, finding an opportunity to tug the ol' peach-colored happy-stick was difficult.

I was never in a fraternity; so homosexual circle jerks were never my thing. It would have been a lot easier if they were.

For example, let me take you back to a specific Friday night, around midnight. I was sitting at my desk, sketching away while everyone else my age was out getting wasted, puking and getting laid. (Not necessarily in that order.) I looked over at Stewart's bed and noticed that he was already sound asleep. *This was my chance. If I didn't take it, I'd miss the window and it would be gone forever. It was go time.*

I clicked off the light over my desk, climbed into bed and pulled the covers up. In a matter of seconds my eyes were closed and I'd managed to free Cobra Commander from my boxer shorts.

Yep, I called my penis Cobra Commander. Got a problem with that? For a while I was thinking about going with Destro, but the shiny silver helmet thing seemed too obvious. *If there's one thing you don't want to be when naming your genitals, it's predictable.*

With Stewart twenty-five penis lengths from me, it wasn't like I could just pop in a porno and go to town. My brain would have to create the necessary images and scenarios. I was counting on it.

I closed my eyes and focused my mind. *Think. Think. Think.*

Suddenly I was in my figure drawing class, but for some reason all of the other male students decided not to show up. It was just me, me and a room full of artsy-fartsy, free-wheeling, open to anything fine art students.

Think. Think. Think.

As luck would have it, the class happened to be without a model and the instructor, who was a looker in her own right, asked if I'd be willing to pose. Who was I to say no?

Think. Think. Think.

I stood and slowly removed my pants, the eyes of every girl in the room singularly fixed on me. When my most private of private areas was at last exposed, a chorus of "oohs" and "ahhs" wafted up from the floor like a thick morning fog. There was even one, "Dear Lord almighty! That thing is massive!" A girl in the back started to fan her face and muttered something along the lines of, "I declare. I do think I'm experiencing a case of the vapors," before she fainted.

Shut up. Don't say a word.

Back in reality, my hand was wrapped around myself and my wrist was moving at lightning speeds beneath the covers. I could literally feel the wonderful babies that lived inside my man sack preparing to begin the glorious orgasm march. It was going to be impressive. It was going to make the *Million Man March* look like a meeting of the David Hyde Pierce Fan Club.

Think. Think. Think.

Back in fantasyland, the girls in the room and the lovely well-preserved instructor had begun to take their clothes off. They surrounded me, drooling at the mouth and licking their lips, converging on me like a pack of hungry penis zombies. You know, minus the whole undead thing. That's a whole different fantasy.

Think. Think. Think.

One especially sexy girl of Mexican descent leaned in close and began nibbling on my ear lobe. Another went to work on my nipple, and another still was teaching herself to drive a stick. There were hands all around me, touching every inch of my flesh. They were licking and kissing and searching for things to rub and squeeze and pull and stro—

BRAFFFFTTTTTTTTTTTTTTTT!

Someone farted.

What the hell? Which one of these morons decided this was the opportune time to rip one?

BRAFFFFFFSSSTTTTTTTTTTTTTT!

Oh hell no! That one was wet! It was wet and it wa — Dear lord, I could smell it! It smelled like burnt macaroni and cheese served up on a corpse during an autopsy! I opened my eyes and the fantasy evaporated in a puff of butt-gaseous smoke. BRAFFFFFFTTTTT-BRAFFTTTTTT-BLUUURRRPPPP! Stewart let another one rip from across the room.

I pulled the covers up and over my nose. Cobra commander began to descent again into his wrinkly skin Terror Dome. For nearly twenty minutes I toyed with the idea of cracking Stewart's skull open with a brick. Unfortunately, there was no brick in the vicinity.

Note to self: Buy more bricks.

THE IDIOT CUT ME OFF

THE IDIOT CUT ME OFF

I was on my way to becoming a sophomore in college, and I was working at the Six Flags Great America theme park in Gurnee, Illinois during the summer months. It had been a particularly long and wildly annoying day of dealing with idiot after idiot and their idiotic offspring. In some cases I also had to put up with the idiotic offspring of the idiotic offspring. *Idiot babies are the worst kind of idiots.*

Despite the cavalcade of idiots, I was required to keep a smile on my face and chipper helpfulness in my voice. Frowning at idiot children or their idiot parents would have resulted in a write up and possibly even a firing by my equally idiotic supervisors.

Having to smile and pretend to keep my knuckles from finding their way into someone's face was difficult. It had a way of making a ten-hour shift seem like a twenty-hour shift and a twenty-hour shift feel like a Tyler Perry movie.

Needless to say, when midnight rolled around and I was leaving the park and saying goodbye to the land of Idiotville, I was pissed off and anxious to get home. I wanted to drop to my pillow and sleep. I wanted to sleep and never wake up. I could see my bed in my mind, all comfy and soft in my nice, quiet, idiot-free room. I pictured myself slowly drifting off to sleep and falling into the reoccurring dream I was having all the time that involved an alien woman from the planet Zarandoz who captured me and forced me to be her love slave.

I loved that dream. She had three boobs, six hands and was a skilled gymnast. She won the bronze at the Space Olympics in 2045 when she finished with a twisting handspring into a six-armed dismount—

SCREECHHHH!

What the hell?

I grabbed hold of the steering wheel and jerked it quickly to the left, narrowly avoiding a car that had just cut me off. *The damn thing missed me by inches!*

I pounded on the wheel with my balled-up fist, leaned forward, pressed my cheek against the windshield and screamed: "Shit! What the fuck, dick head? What do you think you're doing?"

My heart was racing and my lungs were on fire. I almost died! I almost died because some idiot desperately needed to be in my lane when his was perfectly fine! I could feel steam pouring from my ears.

This moron had pushed me over the edge. Without thinking, I leaned my head out the side window and screamed. "You fucking asshole! You dumb fucking asshole! I'm going to fuck your asshole, asshole!"

I really didn't want to fuck his asshole.

I also wasn't sure who exactly I was yelling at. It suddenly dawned on me that whoever was driving that car couldn't hear a word I was saying.

Breathing deeply, I tried my best to relax. Screaming out the window was pointless. It wouldn't accomplish anything. I calmed myself down, slowed my breathing, and even stopped the grinding of my teeth. I needed to forget about Mr. Shit McDrive and move on. I needed to get home and get into bed, and become reacquainted with the three-breasted alien woman in my dreams.

Those boobs would make everything better. *Boobs always make everything better.*

Unfortunately, I failed. No matter how hard I tried to ignore CutOff McCutofferson, the fiery glow of his brake lights refused to leave my field of vision. He was right in front of me, driving along without a care in the world as if nothing ever happened. The lights, those damn, frustrating lights — they were burned into my retinas. They were stuck in the space between my brain and my skull, floating carelessly through the brain fluid with their hands behind their heads while sipping some fruity drink through a straw. They were mocking me.

My three-breasted alien lover disappeared.

I wanted revenge.

Selfish McBreaklights pulled onto the expressway ahead of me. He was headed in the complete opposite direction of me. I followed him anyway. Not only did I follow him, but I continued to follow him for the next forty minutes. When he turned, I turned. When he stopped, I stopped. I had absolutely no idea where I was, or where he was leading me. I really didn't care. For reasons I wasn't entirely sure of, I was following and I didn't want to stop.

Trained detectives didn't follow suspects as well as I was following this schmuck. Scientologists don't follow nonsense as well as I was following him. Cubs fans don't follow losing teams as well as I was following him. Sexually transmitted diseases don't follow Kim Kardashain's vagina as wel— eh, you get my point, right?

When GettingFollowed McJerkAss arrived at his house, I remained hot on his trail. I stopped my car in the middle of the street and left it running. It was at this point that common sense began to settle in. What the hell was I doing? It made no sense. I went an hour out of my way, to an area I was completely unfamiliar with—for what? To scare some jerk that barely wronged me? What if he had a cell phone? What if he noticed me following him and called the cops? *I could go to jail for this.*

Jerkoff McSwitchlanes turned out to be Mrs. Jerkoff McSwitchlanes. The moment she pulled into her driveway she bolted from the car and ran full speed to the front door of her house. After fumbling with the keys for a minute, she managed to get inside and slam the door behind her.

Shit. She must have seen me.

The whole thing did look sort of funny, though. The way she was fumbling with her keys, and breathing heavily. The way she nearly tripped over the shrubs lining the driveway. I started to chuckle.

Until a large man in a white wife beater ran from the house with a baseball bat in his hand and an expression of absolute rage on his face. He was calling me every four letter word in the book and he was headed right for my car. I stopped chuckling.

Slamming on the gas, I drove away like a madman and prayed that neither of them were smart enough to jot down my license number. It took me almost two hours to figure out where I was and make it back home. The world is full of idiots, and apparently I'm one of them.

-Steven Novak-

COUNSELORS, THERAPISTS, AND CUNTS

COUNSELORS, THERAPISTS, AND CUNTS

The bitch ratted me out. It wasn't any of her business, but the bitch ratted me out.

So what if I was drawing pictures of me shooting myself in the head, or hanging myself with a noose, or stabbing myself in the eye with the business end of a spork? So what if I'd scribbled a picture of me slicing my belly open and letting my guts spill out onto the floor where they are being eaten by a pack of rabid dogs? *So what?* How was any of that her business? *It wasn't.*

And yet, the girl sitting next to me during fifth period English in eighth grade, fucking ratted me out. *Cunt.*

I don't even care if the ladies generally don't care much for that word! I don't care if typing it will get me a kick to the groin from every woman I pass on the street! I don't even care if it causes my book to get banned and protesters to line up outside my door! I fucking typed it and I'm not taking it back!

Cunt! Cunt! Cunty cunt cunt!

Okay, so *maybe* it was a mistake to type it *quite* so many times and maybe it'll ruffle the vagina of more than a few of the female readers, but I can't take it back. What's done is done.

Well, wait. I guess I could just go back and erase it.

Naw. Too lazy.

Anyway, the nosey parker sitting next to me told my teacher that she'd seen me drawing and writing suicidal things during class. My nosey teacher told the nosey principal, and the nosey principal told the school counselor. It was this nosey domino effect that began my long and incredibly annoying sojourn into the wonderfully wacky world of therapy.

I'm currently in my early thirties and I've been in therapy for nearly a third of my life. *That's just silly.* What makes the whole thing even sillier is the fact that I can't honestly say I've gotten *anything* from it.

In fact, the only thing therapy has taught me is that I really hate therapy. I hate therapy more than the Twilight books. I hate it more than I hate the people who read the Twilight books. I hate it more than politics, politicians, pedophiles and parachutes. I hate it more than self-esteem. I hate it more than the fact that Paris Hilton spent more money on shoes last month than I'll likely make over the course of my life. *I hate it more than people who make long lists of the things they hate.*

Not only do I hate therapy, I hate therapists as well. They're cunts, plain and simple - even the male ones. The word cunt can cover either gender as far as I'm concerned. I've spilled my guts to six of these so called *professionals* over the years and after only one session with me, five out of six of them arrived at the second appointment and asked me this: "Steven, you wouldn't mind if I started taping recording our sessions, would you?"

God damn it.

Five out of six - can you believe that nonsense?

Am I that messed up? I mean, I know I've lead a *unique* sort of life and I know I've got a few issues to work out, but five out of six? That's the same percentage of dentists that recommend *Oral-B* over any other brand to their patients!

I'd bet dollars to donuts that one of those schmucks has written a paper about me at some point. Maybe they've won an award because of my screwed up, big boob obsessed, G.I. Joe loving, terrified of all things poop-related, full of hatred for all of mankind brain. *Lousy, award-winning cunts.*

By the time I got to college I was so tired and bored of the process of therapy and the utter pointlessness of explaining my feelings that I started blatantly lying to the therapist I was seeing once a week. I was telling her crazy stuff that made no sense and stuff that she honestly shouldn't have believed. I was angry and I was being a jerk.

"So, Steven, how was your weekend?"

"I don't know. Fine I guess."

"Did you try to do what we talked about last week?" She was always giving me little tests designed to force me to interact with my fellow students and occasionally creep from the darkened hole of my apartment.

"You mean, walking up to three people who I don't know and starting a conversation?" *I didn't say they were good tests.*

"Yes. How did you do?"

"I didn't do it."

"And why not?"

"I don't know. I didn't even go to class this week, so I guess that didn't help any."

"Why didn't you go to class?"

"Just didn't feel like it."

"What did you do instead of going to class?"

"Sat around the apartment and masturbated."

"Excuse me?"

"Yeah, I must have masturbated fifty times. Not just in the bed, either. I did it in the bathtub, and on the floors, on the plates in my kitchen, on the door handles…all over."

She paused, and like a well-trained vocalist, she held it. I caught her off guard with my masturbation blurt. She was trying to decide if I was being serious, and if I was being series, she was also trying to figure out the quickest escape route from the office.

It took everything I had in me not to laugh. *Seriously. It wasn't easy.*

Because I'm a jerk and I rarely know when to stop, I continued. "I'm not sure how I got started with it. All I know is that I was watching a documentary on the Napoleonic wars and suddenly I had a hard-on. I'm not sure if it was Napoleon, or his hat, or all the murder and stuff, but it really got me riled up. Do you think that's weird? Is that weird? Is getting an erection because of a hat weird?"

I said nonsense like that to the poor woman every week. Was it mean? No way. *Screw that noise.* She was a therapist and she was getting exactly what she deserved. Serves her right, for trying to help improve my self-esteem and quality of life.

Nosey cunt.

SO THAT'S WHAT THAT LOOKS LİKE İN REAL LİFE

SO THAT'S WHAT THAT LOOKS LIKE IN REAL LIFE

While home from college one summer, I took a job as a security guard at Six Flags Great America in Gurnee, Illinois.

I understand that not everyone has been to a Six Flags, or even heard of it. For those of you unfamiliar, it's basically a mini-Disneyland with more roller coasters. Oh, and replace Mickey Mouse and the gang with Bugs Bunny and the gang. That's pretty much it. Those are the only differences.

Oh, Six Flags is a lot cheaper too. And it's in Gurnee, Illinois, as opposed to Orlando, Florida, which explains why it's so much cheaper.

Every morning I'd drive to work, park, and head "backstage" to get my "costume." We weren't allowed to call it a uniform, or an outfit, or anything else. It was a "costume" and we were expected to call it a "costume." If anyone further up in the Six Flags hierarchy heard it referred to as anything else, someone was getting fired. Seriously, I'm not even joking – people could, and would, and did get fired for exactly that.

My "costume" as a security "specialist" at Six Flags consisted of a blue shirt so tight it hugged, lifted and showcased the curves of my boyish moobs like the world's most supportive bra, and a pair of blue pants so freakishly small that the veins of my penis were clearly visible to anyone willing to take a gander.

Yeah, I just typed the phrase "take a gander." I did that. Me. And I'm under the age of seventy-five. *Go figure.*

Long story short, my "costume" wasn't exactly the height of fashion; in fact, I looked like a real douchebag.

The idea that I was expected to secure anyone or anything while packed into my too-tight get-up was laughable at best. Who in the hell was I supposed to intimidate dressed like that? No one was scared of me and no one was ever going to be scared of me. I was as much an authority figure as Dane Cook is a comedian.

As I left the dressing room every morning, I'd pass by a full-length mirror on the wall just outside the gate leading into the park. *Check your smile.* That's what was written on it. *Check your smile.*

I checked it every day. I never found shit.

Actually I didn't work inside the park, though I still had to pass the mirror. My job was to sit in a little booth at the entrance to the employee parking lot. I was supposed to check for parking permits on the windshields of the cars as they drove by. If the car didn't have one, I'd have to stop them and find out what their business was.

That's what I was supposed to do, anyway, in theory. And if my superior was watching, that's exactly what I did do.

I actually spent most of my time in that booth sitting on my ass (even though I was told repeatedly to remain standing) and sometimes drawing pictures of me doing very bad things to Bugs Bunny on the backs of extra time sheets.

Hey, don't you judge me. Don't you dare judge me with that judging face of yours! Who among us wasn't attracted to Bugs when he was in drag? Who among us didn't lay awake at night wondering exactly what was under the skirt of that pouty-lipped transsexual rabbit? Admit it, when he put that lipstick on, you know you wanted to break off a piece of that. *Just admit it. I won't tell anyone.*

One evening, very late, after the park had closed and the employees had left, I was sitting in my little booth waiting to get the call telling me that I could close up shop and head home for the night. I was sitting on my rear with a wad of crumpled Bugs drawings crammed into my pockets when I heard an unexpected noise.

It was a muffle. *I think.* Maybe a person? *Hard to tell.*

It was night, a little after eleven or so, and it was pretty damn dark. I grabbed my trusty security flashlight and clicked it on. Unfortunately, nothing happened. The batteries were dead. *Great.*

Generally in cases like this I'd simply pretend that I never heard the noise in the first place, go home, crawl into bed and legitimately forget that I heard it at all. If the next day on the morning news I found out that the park had been blown up, I'd just shrug my shoulders like the freeze-frame ending of every terrible 80s sitcom, shake my head, smile, and say, "oops."

For whatever reason, on this specific night, instead of doing nothing, I decided to do something. I was going to investigate. I readjusted my grip on the flashlight (in case I needed to use it as a weapon) and began moving cautiously in the direction of the noise. It was coming from an area just outside the parking lot fence and near a park bench I'd stared at for hours almost every day. With every step, the sounds became more familiar. They were clearer. They were starting to make sense. It was definitely a person. *Two people?*

The closer I drew, the more I could discern visually as well. Someone was on top of the bench. *Wait, no. Three people?* At fifteen feet away the picture had become clearer.

I was right; it was three people, two guys and one girl. The noises I'd heard previously belonged to her and the reason I couldn't quite make them out was simple: her mouth was full of dong. Oh, and there was another one wedged between the folds of her more "special" place from behind.

That's right, on a bench, just outside of Six Flags Great America, at eleven in the evening, these three idiots were going at it like they were on a porno set.

The skinny guy getting the oral satisfaction glanced in my direction and paused for just a fraction of a second before literally leaping ten feet into the air. He tripped over the pants around his ankles, stumbled backward and dropped to his ass. Lady StuffedintheMiddle screamed and rolled off the table. She landed hard on her side, bounced once and managed somehow to seamlessly transition to her feet. The other dude, who was standing to begin with, simply reached down, pulled up his shorts, and took off faster than the Flash that day Batman caught him masturbating in The Justice League war room.

It was sort of like watching drunken geese scatter at the sound of a gunshot. The girl and the guy who was working her from behind scampered off in one direction while the other guy bolted in another. He was heading to the trees, the trees that didn't lead to anything but more trees. *I don't think he had any idea where he was going.*

So what did I do? Not much. Basically, I just stood there and laughed. What the hell did you expect me to do? Chase after them? Tackle them, and wrap arms around their half naked, sex-sweaty bodies and wait for the cops to arrive?

Yeah, right. Think again. If the Six Flags organization had really wanted me to run, they wouldn't have stuffed me into those pants. I wasn't running and tabling anyone in those pants.

Oh, I also went home and masturbated that night. *At least someone had a happy ending.*

PENIS COCK ELLIOT

PENIS COCK ELLIOT

I met my wife of nearly eleven years online.

This was back when meeting people online was even scarier than it is today. In fact, when she flew to Ohio to come face-to-face with me for the first time, most of her friends believed she'd wind up chopped into little pieces, lit on fire and tossed into a dumpster somewhere in Cleveland. (Believe it or not, ending up in Cleveland is actually the worst part of that scenario.)

Instead, she ended up marrying yours truly a little over two years later, which, one could argue, is sort of like dying inside. *So maybe her friends were half right?*

Because she was living in sunny California *(an hour and a half from the hustle and bustle of Los Angeles, an hour from Hollywood, and forty-five minutes from Disneyland)* while I was stuck in the middle of gloomy Ohio *(an hour and a half from some flatlands, an hour from a homeless shelter, and forty-five minutes from the rectum of Indiana)* we were forced to rely on the telephone as our primary means of communication.

This was fantastic in certain ways and terrible in others. It was fantastic because it saved me a boatload of money on romantic dinners and annoying trips to see movies I had no interest in seeing in a vain attempt to woo her into the sack.
It was terrible because it ended up costing me a cruise shipload when it came to phone bills.

The cost of keeping up a cross-country relationship was outrageous back in those days. Keep in mind that this was a good five or six years before Skype and video conferencing, and all those wonderful things that make communication over long distances affordable, was readily available to the masses.

Hell, the internet still relied on your phone line back then. And no, this doesn't make me your grandfather. Technology moves fast, you little bastards. *Now get the hell off my lawn.*

There were times when the wife and I would spend hours chatting. We'd jabber about our respective days. We'd complain about our families. We'd discuss our pasts, and movies, and politics, and music, and food, and television, and television about food — *because Iron Chef discussions are the best kind of discussions.*

Sometimes we would even watch television together, and sometimes we'd try the same foods together, and sometimes we'd try watching the same television about foods together, *because Iron Chef watching while eating is alwa—* Sigh. That joke is already old.

No matter what we watched or chatted about, our conversations would almost always end with something along the lines of "Love you. Talk to you later."

It was a classic goodbye. It had dignity and honor, and kings and queens and paupers alike had uttered it, for generations.

At the same time, it was, admittedly, a bit predictable. So I decided to mix things up. "Love you."

"Love you too."

"Talk to you later, Putz McGee."

There was a pause. "What?"

"I said, I'll talk to you later, Putz McGee."

Even at this stage in our relationship my wife-to-be knew I was an idiot. The fact that random, nonsensical gibberish was spewing from my mouth wasn't exactly a new development. I'd been doing it since the first time we spoke and I was going to spend the next forty years repeating it. I'm going to do it on her deathbed. *She'll be annoyed.*

My future bride sighed deeply and took it in stride. "Okay. Talk to you later."

The next time we talked, I took it my new goodbye-greeting a step further. "Love you."

"Love you too."

"Talk to you later, Putz McGee, CCAD."

Again came the pause. "Did you just say Putz McGee, CCAD?"

CCAD was the abbreviation for the college I was attending.

"Yeah. So?"

"Why?"

"Why not?" *She couldn't argue with that kind of logic.*

The next time we spoke, much to my surprise, she decided to get in on the *fun*. "Love you, Steven."

"Love you too."

"Talk to you later, Putz McGee, CCAD, Penis." *Penis, huh? Fresh.*

"Penis, huh?"

"That's what I said."

It went on like this for months. We went back and forth, each of us adding something new onto the end of what was quickly becoming an idiotically long sign-off.

"Talk to you later, Putz McGee, CCAD, penis, cock, Elliot, what's up chicken butt, thumb butt, Terrycloth Johnson."

The additions were getting weirder and weirder. Some of them made sense in the context of the day's conversation and some of them (mostly mine) were little more than random brain farts and diarrhea mouth-drool.

"Talk to you later, Putz McGee, CCAD, penis, cock, Elliot, what's up chicken butt, thumb butt, Terrycloth Johnson, Pecos Bill, throwing rocks and pitching woo, old socks and eating gruel, keep it real, keep it false, keep it around, a hat on a mouse."

Before long it was becoming hard to remember everything. When one of us would get something mixed up or forget a word, the other would immediately call them out.

"Sorry, you forgot to say thumb butt."

"Damn it!"

Eventually the length of our moronic goodbye became so absurd that I had to keep it written on a slip of paper beside my bed. Every time we added something new, I updated it immediately.

"Love you."

"Love you too."

"Talk to you later, Putz McGee, CCAD, penis, cock, Elliot, what's up chicken butt, thumb butt, Terrycloth Johnson, Pecos Bill, throwing rocks and pitching woo, old socks and eating gruel, keep it real, keep it false, keep it around, a hat on a mouse, morning afternoon and night, lovers' delight, I hate you, I hate you too, mixed martial arts, Mark Coleman wears shoes, wrestling, bamboo, tiny underpants, smiles and laughs, tickle and punch, kick and scratch."

The Mark Coleman reference was a particular favorite of mine.

It would take us ten minutes to say goodbye and every goodbye was preceded by an exasperated sigh. What had started as a cute little thing that proved we were meant for each other had transformed very quickly into something nauseating.

"Love you."

"Love you too."

"Talk to you later, Putz McGee, CCAD, penis, cock, Elliot, what's up chicken butt, thumb butt, Terrycloth Johnson, Pecos Bill, throwing rocks and pitching woo, old socks and eating gruel, keep it real, keep it false, keep it around, a hat on a mouse, morning afternoon and night, lovers' delight, I hate you, I hate you too, mixed martial arts, Mark Coleman wears shoes, wrestling, bamboo, tiny underpants, smiles and laughs, tickle and punch, kick and scratch, shoe rack, butt crack, crusted with cheese, deli sandwich, hair pie manwich, snort cocaine, shooting drugs, Willy Wonka's chocolate factory, Augustus was a jerk."

Augustus really was a jerk.

We could have said enough is enough and stopped. We could have called it quits and crumpled up our respective lists and tossed them in the trash. We could have even attached our white pillowcases to broom handles and signaled our surrender. In fact, we probably should have. Too bad that's not what we did.

"Love you."

"Love you too."

"Talk to you later, Putz McGee, CCAD, penis, cock, Elliot, what's up chicken butt, thumb butt, Terrycloth Johnson, Pecos Bill, throwing rocks and pitching woo, old socks and eating gruel, keep it real, keep it false, keep it around, a hat on a mouse, morning afternoon and night, lovers' delight, I hate you, I hate you too, mixed martial arts, Mark Coleman wears shoes, wrestling, bamboo, tiny underpants, smiles and laughs, tickle and punch, kick and scratch, shoe rack, butt crack, crusted with cheese, deli sandwich, hair pie manwich, snort cocaine, shooting drugs, Willy Wonka's chocolate factory, Augustus was a jerk, measles, mumps, urinary tract infection, fallopian tubes filled with goo, I hate mules, I like mules, Iron Chef Morimoto, Iron Chef Sakai, mushroom basil titty-tarts, rock salt cheese toasts, porterhouse steak and butter-soaked talon twisters, creepy mustache man, likes lovin' in a can, trash can, hobo fires, smell like biscuits and raccoon tails."

Eventually the insanity came to a stop. My lovely lady phone pal had had enough. She told me that she just couldn't do it anymore. It would very literally take us ten minutes to say goodbye near the end of our run.

I kept the paper I'd used for notes and for the briefest of moments actually considered using it as my vows at our wedding. I wasn't entirely sure how her family would take the term *"hair pie manwich"* though. Probably not well.

TALES OF PEPSI AND THE MENTALLY CHALLENGED

TALES OF PEPSI AND THE MENTALLY CHALLENGED

The job of a "Driver Helper" at the Pepsi Bottling Company is to *aid the driver in his or her daily deliveries* - at least that's what they say when they hire you.

In truth, the job of a "Driver Helper" at the Pepsi Bottling Company is to *get pushed around by the driver, and do any and all of the physical work while the driver sits on his backside in the truck and stuffs his face with a disgusting day old chicken sandwich he picked up "fresh" at the 7-Eleven.*

Working for Pepsi sucked. It sucked hard. It sucked like a lady of the night with a mouthful of shattered teeth after a particularly stiff pimp slap the night before. It sucked awkward and it sucked sloppy. It sucked like Madonna's acting career and Madonna's singing career. *It also sucked like Madonna's fake English accent.*

Five days of the week I'd work anywhere from a twelve to a fourteen-hour day. On Saturdays I worked a solid eight hours and was expected to travel to four sometimes local and sometimes not so local stores to merchandise the product.

On top of it all, the pay was essentially peanuts. Don't get me wrong, in the grand scheme of things I ended up making decent money, but it was only because of the incredible hours I was putting in. Drivers made a killing. Driver Helpers got pooped on. I'm talking about sticky poop, the kind of poop that requires a folded piece of toilet paper and a second or third swipe before things even begin to get clean.

The drivers at Pepsi liked me, for the most part. They never went out of their way to invite me to any barbeques or birthday parties or anything, but they appreciated that I never complained and broke my back day in and day out.

They even gave me a nickname: *The Mule*. I always assumed it was because I worked as hard as one. I suppose it could have been because they assumed I was as dumb as one for working as hard as one. *It would have been sweet if it were because I was hung like one, but something tells me that wasn't the case.*

I delivered to a lot of weird places while working for Pepsi; bars, offices, grocery stores in good parts of town, and some in the not so good.

In a couple towns, it was required that one of us remain outside to guard the truck while the other went in, which I thought was pretty silly. I wasn't going to guard a bunch of bottles of Pepsi. *It just wasn't going to happen.* If someone wanted to steal something, they were going to steal it. If they threatened me with violence I would have helped them load it into their car.

The first driver I ever rode with either forgot this most golden of golden rules, or had never heard of it in the first place. When we came out of the store, a couple of sneaky hoodlums had worked their way into the truck and were loading cases of soda into their trunk. My driver growled. He dropped his clipboard and ran at them, screaming and waving his fists in the air like a madman. The low-level thieves hopped in their car and sped away. I couldn't help but chuckle. When my driver threw a bottle of Mountain Dew at their car and it slammed off the back windshield, exploded, and went flying fifty feet in the opposite direction, I laughed my ass off. *You would have too.*

There was one place in particular though, a place I dreaded delivering to more than any other. It wasn't in a bad neighborhood and it wasn't even a huge delivery that required a lot of work on my part.

It was *Lambs Farm*, in Libertyville, Illinois.

What's that? Never heard of it? Well, here's a snippet from their website: "*Founded in 1961, Lambs Farm is a premier non-profit organization serving adults with developmental disabilities. Lambs Farm has grown from a small pet shop in Chicago to a 72-acre campus located in Libertyville, Illinois where opportunity flourishes for the more than 250 men and women served.*"

Lambs Farm is a really, really fantastic idea and I have nothing but respect for the good work they're doing. I want to make that perfectly clear. It's a truly wonderful place, run by big-hearted, fantastic people. The world needs more *Lambs Farms*.

That being said, holy Toledo it was annoying to deliver there.

On my very first delivery to Lambs Farm, the driver went in to do whatever it was he did, while I started getting together the order from the truck. I stacked my dolly full and entered through the back of the building.

Out of the corner of my eye I noticed something charging in my direction. It was big and it was coming quick, and it wasn't stopping. "I'll help!" It was a mentally handicapped kid with a dolly of his own. He was charging at me like a pick-up truck with a drunken drunkard, drunked up on drunken drink behind the wheel.

From somewhere behind me, a worried voice screamed, "Phillip, no!"

I tried to move, but I was lugging around two hundred pounds of sugary fizz drink and my reaction time was noticeably labored. The kid slammed right into my leg with the sharp edge of his dolly and I crumbled. Instinctively I reached for my leg, fearing I'd been sliced open. I lost control of my dolly. It flopped forward and spilled across the floor. Bottle caps exploded, plastic ripped open and suddenly the bottles were spinning like tops on the ground and shooting soda in every direction.

Someone nearby screamed, "Oh, Jesus, not again!"

The woman and a few volunteers gathered round, trying their best to corral the kids who were suddenly splashing in the puddles and jumping around in the soda spraying like a sprinkler in Wonka's Chocolate factory. I was drenched, I was sticky, and my shin was bleeding.

Stuff like this happened each and every time I delivered there. Ten-year-old kids in the bodies of twenty-year-old men would steal soda and run away with it for no apparent reason. Sticky-faced thirty-somethings still struggling with the concept of two plus two would talk my ear off for hours about the most inane and incomprehensible things.

There was even a kid who loved to throw pens at me. Yep, the dude would bounce them off my skull whenever he felt like it and he'd do it with the same precision that blew Kennedy's brains all over Jackie O's pretty green dress. He seemed to believe I was a walrus, but he could hit my ear in the exact same spot every damn time. *Go figure.*

What was I supposed to do? Get pissed at them? Start screaming and throw some things, and call them names? *Granted, I'm sometimes a douchebag, but not that big a douchebag.*

I hated delivering to *Lambs Farm*. Scratch that – truthfully, I just hated working for Pepsi. It got me into shape and I managed to get a pretty decent tan by the end of the summer, but neither of those things ever got me laid. So, yeah, I hated Pepsi.

THE PERFECT WAY TO TELL A GIRL YOU LOVE HER

THE PERFECT WAY TO TELL A GIRL YOU LOVE HER

My wife Tami and I met online when I was a senior in College. She lived in California and I was going to school in Ohio. With half the country between us, we spent hours upon hours on the phone, all day, every day. The obsession came quickly and the obsession stuck. Suddenly she was missing work. Suddenly my assignments were late. The lack of sleep turned us into zombies: love zombies, sure, but zombies nonetheless.

I suppose it was all worth it though, right? I mean, I'm happily married to this very day because of those confusing late night love zombie discussions. *So that means it was worth it, doesn't it?*

She does watch MTV way more than she should, though, and I think she has a Britney Spears song on her iPod. *Maybe I should rethink this whole thing.*

Anyway, after months of chitchat and chatter and chatter-chit, our conversations inevitably led to sex. It had to happen sooner or later. We were normal, healthy human beings and we were feeling the sexual frustration that comes with the package deal of a long distance relationship.

Speaking of packages. "I think I have a fairly sizable penis." That was me, responding to a question asked by her a moment before.

"Fairly sizable? Steven, why do you always have to talk like that?" That was her, responding to my answer with a sigh so animated I could almost see her shaking her head six states away.

"What do you mean, what's wrong with fairly sizable?"

"Nothing, I guess. It's not really the *sexiest* response, though. It sounds nerdy. It's something a nerd would say."

"But it's how I talk."

She sighed again. "I know it is...believe me, I know it is."

At that moment I was struck with an idea. Actually, hit with an idea would be more appropriate phrasing. The idea in question was so amazingly incredible, so mind-blowingly awesome and so bonkers unique that it smacked me like an aluminum bat to the face swung by Big Foot himself. Big Foot is a pretty strong dude - at least, according to the stories of the drunken hillbillies claiming to have seen him. *Who am I to doubt the word of a liquored up old fart that makes passionate love to his sheep as much as his wife?*

So what was my idea? Well, I was going to make it possible for my long-distance lover to actually see my penis. How was I going to pull that off? I was going to sculpt an exact replica and send it to her.

It was a fantastic plan — or at least it sounded like a fantastic plan when it popped into my head at the time. *Typing it the way I just did and reading it back to myself years later makes me wonder exactly what the hell I was thinking.*

There are so very few things about myself worthy of a brag, a humble brag, or even a passing mention without hanging my head in shame. I'm a dork. I don't drink. I don't go to parties. I don't make a ton of money. My looks are average to below average at best. My clothes are old. My personality is crummy. My jokes are terrible. I'm an absolute mess when it comes to the social graces. I'm the world's greatest party pooper. My personal hygiene is questionable and I sometimes break wind when I do a sit-up. I'm essentially a cranky sixty-year-old man in the body of a thirty-three year-old and on top of it all, I still read comic books and I still collect G.I. Joes.

Whew.

The point I'm trying to make is that I'm a walking bag of pathetic. My penis though - I'm okay with my penis.

Don't get me wrong; it's not crazy-enormous or anything. Women don't pass out when they see it and the citizens of Tokyo don't scream in terror when it attacks the city. It's not bad though. It's *fairly sizable.*

Anxious to show off just how fairly sizable, I went out and purchased myself a box of artist modeling clay called "*Super Sculpy.*" Super Sculpy is pretty much exactly like regular old clay, except for the fact that it never dries out and you can fire the finished product in your home oven.

This was important because I had no intention of showing up at school with a big ol' clay wang in my hand and asking to use the kiln. *I don't imagine that request would have been well received.*

That very same night I sat down at my desk and started sculpting. I was sculpting a penis: a replica penis of my own penis. Needless to say, I made sure the blinds were closed before starting.

It took me thirty minutes to work out a basic shape, but I wasn't completely positive about the size. Not to brag or anything, but it seemed a little too big. For reasons I won't dare attempt to explain, my representation should be completely and totally accurate. I wanted every vein represented and every curve showcased. I wasn't making a piece of art as much as working out a mathematical equation. I wanted her to know what to expect, and what she was getting herself into and what would be getting into her. *Basically I was being an idiot.*

It's because of this desire for utmost realism that I went into the bathroom, washed the excess clay dust off my hands, popped in a pornographic movie, returned to my desk, and dropped my britches. I also grabbed a ruler and a pencil. *When I called myself an idiot, I was being overly generous.*

Over the course of the next twenty minutes, I worked myself up to the peak of excitement. My man parts were engorged and pulled tight and as big as they were ever going get. Then I stopped. It was hard (pun intended), but I stopped. I grabbed my ruler, made my measurements, and jotted them down before snagging Sculpy penis and doing a visual comparison.

They were actually pretty damn close.

The leftish curve wasn't exactly right, but that was easily correctable. Truthfully, I was kind of proud of myself, which is both sad and disturbing. I mean, there I was, in my apartment, naked, with a flesh and blood penis in one hand and a clay replica in the other. *It wasn't exactly the sort of image that makes it onto the Christmas cards.*

That night I fired my Sculpy penis in the oven and checked it repeatedly like a baker waiting for a soufflé to rise. I packaged the package the next very day and sent it to my future wife. That night I called her on the phone. "Hey, you'll never guess what I sent to you in the mail today."

"What?"

"No. I'm not telling. You have to guess."

"I don't know, flowers?"

"Way better than flowers...flowers times ten."

"What?"

"Come on, just one more guess."

"Steven, I'm not going to sit here all night and guess. Just tell me."

"Fine. What would you say if I told you it was a completely accurate sculpture of my penis?"

You could have heard a pin drop. *You could have heard a pin drop somewhere in New Jersey - all the way from Africa.*

"What?"

"Last night I sculpted my penis. I sent it to you this morning."

"You sent me a clay penis?"

"Yep."

"What? What's the matter with you? Why would you do that?"

"Oh, wait. Was that not *sexy* enough? I mean my cock. I sculpted my cock out of clay and sent it to you."

It really is a wonder that this woman actually ended up marrying me.

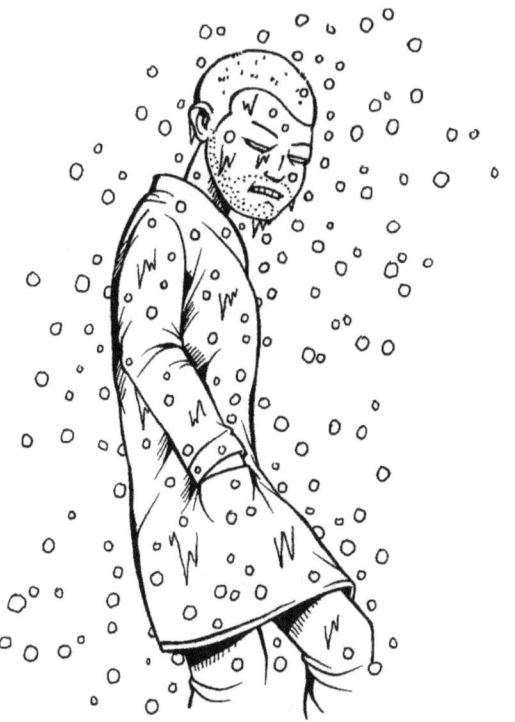

WENDY'S AT 9AM?

WENDY'S AT 9AM?

"You know what would really hit the spot right about now?"

"I don't know, what?"

"Some Wendy's."

"Wendy's?"

"Yeah. Don't you think it's the perfect time for Wendy's?"

"No. Not really. It's like…nine in the morning."

"Yeah, I know. But, still. It would taste good."

The dolt requesting a greasy hamburger at 9AM was my future wife. She'd flown out from California to visit me a few days earlier and was staying with me at my apartment in the city.

The night before had gone well. We did the *dinner* thing. We did the *movie* thing. I tried my best to do my own version of the *romance* thing and to top it all off, I even gave the whole *sweet lovin'* thing a go. While I didn't do any of those things particularly well individually, lumped together in a big date night stew, I like to think the whole proved better than the sum of its parts.

Maybe. Maybe not.

In any case, it was the next morning, I'd just woken up and the lovely-insane bastard beside me was insisting that a sloppy, grease-ridden burger from Wendy's would "hit the spot."

She'd obviously gone bonkers.

Wendy's? Really? At nine in the morning? She had to be joking.
What sort of screwed up screwhole eats a Wendy's hamburger at nine in the morning? Even Dave Thomas wouldn't do that. Even the corpse of Dave Thomas wouldn't do that.

I'm not even kidding. If you tried to wedge a piping hot bacon cheeseburger between his decaying choppers, he'd spit that garbage right out.

To make matters worse, I looked out the window and noticed that it was pouring freezing rain. It was early December in Ohio, and it was raining. *It was frostbite weather. It was stay outside and lose your toes weather.* She must have been off her rocker if she thought for a second that I would walk five blocks through the city in that nonsense.

Intent on keeping the peace, I offered something else instead. "Can't I just make you eggs or something? Don't eggs sound good? Wouldn't it be cool if I made some eggs for you?"

"I'd really like Wendy's." *Damn it.*

I tried to sweeten the pot. "Tell you what…I'll make them naked. How about that? Naked eggs? Come on. You're not going to sit there and turn down naked eggs, are you?"

"Sorry. I just have a taste for Wendy's." *Double damn it.*

"It's like fifteen below zero out there, and it's raining. Ice. You see the ice rain, right?"

"I know. It would mean a lot to me, though." *Shit.*

This broad wasn't going to let this go. She was set on the idea of Wendy's and she wasn't going to budge. Even the promise of naked eggs couldn't turn her away. *Naked eggs!*

I suppose if I were blessed with a larger set of balls and wasn't such a pushover when it came to women who were willing to let me even suggest naked eggs without slapping on a restraining order, I would have explained to her in no uncertain terms that Wendy's simply wasn't in the cards. *I am a pushover though.* I'm a pushover and a schmuck, and ten minutes later I was bundled up in a winter jacket and leaving my building like the schmucky, pushover, no-balled schmuck that I'd always be. *Naked eggs would have been so much more fun.*

The wind was blowing like an angry working girl after a twelve-hour shift. It didn't like me and I didn't like it, but neither of us was going anywhere. Icy cold rain stabbed me in the face like knives, or a million cheek pinches from a million annoying aunts all at once.

The sidewalks were coated and shimmering and slippery. Every step was a cautious one. Every movement had to be carefully planned and tested before completed. A single car drove slowly by, and the person inside looked at me like I was a crazy man. *They had no idea.*

By the time I arrived at Wendy's, frostbite had set in and my fingers were utterly useless. My jaw was clattering. There were icicles hanging off my eyebrows and my eyelids were frozen open. Blinking was no longer an option. I couldn't feel my ears. For all I knew, they'd fallen off along the way.

I'd transformed into Brundle fly. *I was falling apart.* The worst thing about it –I still had to go back.

She just had to have Wendy's! No! Naked eggs weren't good enough for Princess California! She had to have Wendy's and she required me to put my life on the line to get it! She asked me to undertake a journey that put the trek to Modor to shame!

Tomorrow morning she was getting eggs. And not even naked eggs. *She blew her chance at naked eggs.*

Fifteen minutes later I stumbled into the apartment with a bag of Wendy's in what was essentially a block of ice. "Here you go…Wendy's. Let me just say, this better be the best damn Wendy's you've ever eaten considering what I went through to get it for you."

She lowered her head, ashamed. *Damn straight.*

"I'm sorry Steven. I'm not even really hungry."

Wait. What?

"What the hell? Then what did you send me to Wendy's for?"

"I had to use the bathroom."

"Huh?"

"I had to use the bathroom, and I didn't want to do it with you in the apartment."

The next time I make naked eggs I'm lacing them with poison.

-Steven Novak-

HOW ABOUT A CRUISE?

HOW ABOUT A CRUISE?

For our honeymoon, my wife and I decided we would take a cruise to Mexico. We didn't want to spend a ton of money because we were saving for a house and neither of us had ever been on a cruise so we figured, why not Mexico? Mexico and a cruise ship for three days might be fun, right?

I mean, what could be more enjoyable than repeatedly stuffing our bellies with buffet food on a floating city before docking and spending the day taking in the sights of and sounds of Mexico while malnourished, overworked children tried their damndest to sell us boxes of Chiclets? If you can't enjoy rubbing your overfed gut in the faces of the suffering masses, then you're probably an unhappy party-pooper who can't enjoy anything.

Did the sarcasm come through there? I really hope it came through, otherwise your opinion of me most likely dropped right off the map.

Having never been on the ocean, or really even on a boat for that matter, the wife and I had no idea what to expect before we stepped onto the cruise ship to begin our grand belly-stuffing adventure. She was worried the ship was going to sink. I was worried we were going to get really bored.

Neither of us had it right.

A couple weeks before leaving, my mother told me over the phone that I should consider the possibility of taking a seasickness pill before we boarded. I pretended to take her suggestion seriously and openly mocked her after hanging up. *A seasickness pill? Seriously?*

She had no idea who she was talking to. If she did, she never would have suggested it. I was Steven-MOTHERFUCKING-Novak. (With the MOTHERFUCKING in caps because of my extra manliness.) I didn't need any stupid seasickness pills. Seasickness pills were for grandmas and little girls, and guys who have tracks from Cabaret on their iPods.

Seasickness pills - whatever, mom. Let me just jot that suggestion of yours down in my imaginary notebook with my imaginary pen. Idiot.

Our very first night on the boat, the wife and I were sitting in the dining room, and we were all dressed up, and looking as sharp as two people unaccustomed to being dressed up could possibly look. We were relaxing; we were chatting and laughing, and wide-eyed and ready to make the most out of our honeymoon. Things were going well. This was the start of our lives together as husband and wife and we were damn sure going to make the most of it.

Oh, we were also ready to get down to some serious open seas marital relations later in the afternoon. I was really looking forward to humping to the rhythm of the dolphin-song outside. *I like to think the dolphins were looking forward to it too.*

Everything was going great and our grand marriage adventure was going to be fantastic, or at least it seemed that way—for a moment.

Suddenly the dining room seemed to be bouncing a bit more than it had been a moment prior. Suddenly my head felt both light and heavy, and heavy-light. I felt like I was going up in a hot air balloon immediately after Thanksgiving dinner. I lazily glanced at a waiter across the room and could swear he was bouncing around on springs attached to the soles of his shoes. My eyes rolled into my head. My tongue flopped out of my mouth and hung over my lower lip like wet laundry. I pressed my knuckles into my eye sockets and pushed back so far that I was massaging the gray matter of my brain.

My wife took note of the fact that my skin was flushed and my breathing labored. "Steven, are you okay?"

I couldn't look her straight in the face. She was swaying side to side and she was doing it in slow motion. Her face was stretching, the edges were slowly folding into the background and evaporating like sugar crystals in a glass of tea.

"Steven?" Every time she said my name I felt like there was a power drill screwing its way into my temple.

My response was unintelligible. "Yeah. Yeah, I'm fine. Just...doing...stuff..."

"You don't look fine."

"Yeah, I don't know. It's just—all of a sudden..."

Something in my stomach lurched. Something else in my throat gurgled. Something in the rear of my mouth decided to take a dump on the gurgling in my throat and the lurching in my stomach. (I believe it's called an upper-decker.) Within moments the lurching and the gurgling and crap-coated awfulness began moving upward.

I said exactly what I was feeling. "Oh, shit."

"What? What is it, Steven? Are you okay? What?"

My hand immediately went to my mouth in order to keep the barroom brawl inside me from spilling into the streets. Despite my wobbly legs, I forced myself to stand. "I think I need to go back to the room."

"What? Are you sure? What's wrong?"

I made the mistake of looking down at the floor and noticed it was wobbling like a bowl of Jello. It looked slippery. It looked wet and dangerous, and I suddenly wasn't so sure I'd be able to navigate it.

Before my wife could even weigh in on the idea of calling it a night, I was already moving through the dining room, carefully avoiding waiters and travelers like the pixilated frog from the old Frogger game, minus the kick ass soundtrack.

Seven minutes later I was hunched over the toilet with my insides violently spewing from my mouth and minuscule particles of splash-back spraying across the bathroom floor.

Looking back on it now, the only saving grace of the whole situation—from my perspective, anyway—was the fact that five hours later my wife was doing the same. *Being seasick is a lot more fun when you can share it with someone.*

On my honeymoon there were very few smiles. There were very few laughs, and there was absolutely no steamy intercourse to the sensual cries of the dolphins outside.

There was only puke and more puke. Then there was a little more puke on top of that.

Goats Eat Cans Volume 2

MY WIFE TELLS SOME PISS POOR STORIES

MY WIFE TELLS SOME PISS POOR STORIES

I love my wife and I'd do absolutely anything for her. She's beautiful, she's intelligent, she's funny, and sometimes she smells like pears. Her mere presence in my life makes me think I actually might be worth a damn, and that there's a possibility, however faint, that I could be something other than completely useless. I'd marry her a thousand times over if I could.

That being said, the woman could not tell an interesting story if her life depended on it. Seriously, if some random-hooded thug had a gun to her head and told her to tell him an interesting story or he'd blow the head clear off her shoulders, well, let's just say I'd be scrubbing her blood off the carpet and picking pieces of her brain out from our stucco walls.

What? You think that was mean of me? You believe I might have gone a little too far with the whole "brains in stucco" thing?

Well, you're wrong. Honestly, I didn't go far enough.

To better illustrate my point, I ask you now to follow along as I give you an example of the type of conversations my wife and I have on a fairly regular basis.

"So how was work today, T?"

That was me. I was doing the good *husbandly* thing and asking my wife how her day was. I used to ask this question a lot when we were first married because I loved her and I was genuinely interested in hearing how she spent the hours we were apart.

I don't ask it so much anymore – for reasons that will soon become clear.

She'd usually pep up upon hearing this question. Her eyes would get big and her smile would widen. It's the same expression a puppy makes when you offer it a piece of cheese or the leftovers from the morning breakfast.

"Really?"

"Yeah, of course. What happened today? How'd everything go?"

When she said "Really?" I should have responded with, "No, of course not. I'd have to be an idiot to seriously want to put myself through that," but I didn't. Hindsight is a mean son of a bitch. Hindsight is that kid you knew growing up that had a bike, while you were still scooting around in your stupid, plastic Big Wheel. *Hindsight likes to rub shit in your face.*

As she started her story, she was all smiles and butterscotch. She had stuff she wanted to tell me and she was anxious to tell it. "Well, today we had an IEP meeting about Martin. His parents and their advocate were there, and you know it's really important that parents have an advo-cate...there...be—"

As quickly as she started, she was fading away.

The upward curls on the corners of her lips flattened. The stack of bills in her hands had garnered her attention. There was an electric bill, a cell phone bill, a credit card bill, a thank you card for the mostly awful gift we bought my brother and his wife for their wedding shower. There was too much for her to look at and take in. It was sensory overload, and she was unable to stay focused. In a matter of seconds she'd stopped talking altogether.

I tried to bring her back. "Hun?" For a moment, anyway, it worked.

"Oh? What? Oh...yeah...so...what was I talking about?"

"Something about Martin and IEP or something like that…"

"Oh, yeah, yeah! Oh! You'll never believe what Lisa told me about Janice and Debbie Menn!"

I had no idea who Janice was, or Debbie Menn for that matter. Neither of these facts were of interest to her. Everyone knows background information is a wildly overrated aspect of storytelling, anyway.

"So, anyway, it turns out Debbie has been having an affair with Lewis. You know Lewis, right? Lewis who teaches fifth grade…you know him."

I had no idea who Lewis was either, despite her insistence to the contrary.

"Well, I guess they've broken it off now and…then…there was some…other…stuff…"

Shit. She'd finished flipping through the bills, tossed them aside and moved onto her fingers. She was examining the nails and picking at the polish, and seemed absolutely absorbed in the process. "I can't believe how bad my fingers look. Can you believe this? I broke this nail at work today…"

In less than three minutes she'd managed to change subjects no less than three times. *That's a subject a minute for all the math geniuses out there.* Her complete lack of focus was astounding. If someone, somewhere happened to be offering up an award for lack of focus *(possibly called The Focuseys)* she would have been a shoe-in to walk away with a statuette of some sort

I think my wife's brain might look a lot like a scene from Hitchcock's *The Birds*. I imagine thoughts and ideas flying around, slamming into each other without rhyme or reason, chirping and squawking and leaving piles of Oreo cookie colored poop all over the place. *I bet it makes for one hell of a CAT Scan.*

"Hey! Don't let me forget! I need to call your mother and ask her how formal the Christmas dinner is going to be."

Holy crap. She actually finished a thought. With the examination of her broken nails and painted fingers apparently completed, she actually managed to construct something resembling a partially coherent thought. The sentence had a beginning and an ending, and it even called on me to participate in the conversation on some level. This was a remarkable change of events.

If I had a big red marker handy I would've drawn a smiley face on the calendar or something. At the very least she deserved a gold star, or maybe a rainbow sticker or som—

"What's on TV tonight? Is it "Project Runway?" *Ooh. Spoke too soon.*

She switched conversations so quickly it gave me whiplash. I could have sued, but we were married. Her money was my money and I would have just been suing myself.

With a heavy sigh and a shake of my head, I turned to walk away.

"Hey! Where are you going?"

"Upstairs. I suddenly have a really good idea for a story."

"Wait! Wait!" She snagged her purse with one hand and tossed it in my direction. "Can you do me a favor and take this with you. Just put it by the thing…in the room…"

"The thing in what room?"

"You know, the thing on the desk. The gumanta."

Gumanta? I didn't respond, because there was no response.

"You know what I'm talking about. Just put it by the magic music maker, Steven."

She was talking about the little radio in the bathroom – or maybe the alarm clock. Don't ask me how I figured it out. I didn't bother to narrow it down.

As I was about to leave the room she stopped me again. "What's it about?"

"What's what about?"

"Your story."

"It's about how you can't tell a good story."

"What are you talking about? I tell great stories! Just today I was telling Angie about this one time when…she…and then some…thing…else…"

She was flipping though the channels on the television and slowly fading away once again. It was 4:15 and Judge Judy was on. The old broad was telling some kid to stop pissing on her leg and calling it rain, or something equally idiotic. Whatever it was, my wife found it hilarious.

Content that our *conversation* had concluded, I headed upstairs. I'm not entirely convinced she even knew I left. I had a story to write – *you know, after a quick stop at the magic music maker, of course.*

THE ANGRY DUDE IN MY STOMACH IS NAMED BIFF

THE ANGRY DUDE IN MY STOMACH IS NAMED BIFF

I love pizza.

When I say that I love pizza, I mean I really love it. I love it so much I want to drop my pants, slide out of my undies and make sweet, sweet love to it. When I'm done making love to it, I want to screw it. *Pizza likes it rough too.*

Pizza is better than winning the lottery. It's better than *Star Trek* and it's better than *Star Trek: The Next Generation*. Pizza is better than mom's homemade apple pie. It's better than winning the Super Bowl, and it's a hell of a lot better than winning the U.S. Open. Pizza is better than crack and cocaine, and it's better than butter-soaked biscuits and jam resting on the tanned buttocks of a bikini-clad Rosario Dawson. Pizza is better than oral sex.

Wait, scratch that and revise. Pizza is better than an hour-long session of oral sex skillfully administered by three women at once, all of whom have been trained, tested and universally certified in the fine art of oral sex.

This story is about one night with one pizza from a nearby joint called Rosito's.

I'd swallowed the last of the deliciously gooey slices thirty minutes prior and unfortunately, something was wrong. The cheesy goodness wasn't quite sitting right. My stomach felt twisted. It was moving and morphing, and wrenching and tying itself into knots, and it was doing it slowly. My insides were belching and my backside was puffing. The awful sensation sloshing inside my knotted stomach was slowly progressing upward. It was heading for the light of my mouth.

My wife noticed my discomfort and managed to pull her attention from what I'm sure was a *fantastic* episode of *Keeping Up With the Kardashians* long enough to make sure I wasn't dying. "Steven, are you all right?"

There was a pissed off little person trapped in my belly. His name was Biff. He was wearing overalls, a hard hat, and he was working a jackhammer against my slippery, boiling interior while smoking a comically oversized cigar and letting the ashes pool in my stomach acids.

Of course I wasn't all right. *I was nowhere near all right.*

It's a little-known fact that three-foot tall dudes named Biff are undoubtedly the angriest three-foot tall people of all. *You can take that to the bank.*

In between a stingy hot series of acid-soaked belches, I managed to tell my wife that I was going to hop in the shower. I needed to do something, anything. I was feeling light-headed and I could taste the metal aftermath of bile across the surface of my tongue. I thought maybe the water would make me feel better. *It made sense in my head.*

I wobbled into the bathroom, turned on the water, slid out of my clothes and hopped in. At first it was working. The water felt good. It was warm and it gave me something else to focus on. I leaned my head against the tile, closed my eyes and tried my damndest to relax. I swallowed a mouthful of water and let in land on Biff's head.

He'd been working the night shift. He was grimy, he was coated in the scent of cigar smoke, and he was in desperate need of a shower. I thought he might appreciate it. For a moment, the gruff old bastard laid down his jackhammer and stopped chopping away at my insides.

I sighed and smiled. I'd done it. Everything was going to be okay.

Or was it?

Fresh and clean, energized and ready to roll, Biff popped another stogie into his mouth and lit it up. *Everything wasn't going to be okay.*

My insides flipped. My stomach exploded and something that smelled like fried death popped like an over-inflated sex doll from between my lips. Less than a second later my insides were sprinting toward my mouth. A of river bile was shooting upward, chunks of pizza cheese and sloppy dough mixed like spawning salmon among the waves. I keeled over. I couldn't help it.

It felt like someone had kicked me in the stomach. Choice and thought were a thing of the past. This was reaction and nothing else. I was at the mercy of the Biff and his jackhammer, and the volcano of nastiness frothing within. My mouth opened and began to spray.

It was lumpy liquid awful.

In mere seconds I'd transformed into a pasty, naked, fire-breathing dragon. My throat heaved and my mouth erupted. Chunks of four different cheeses, perfectly seasoned dough, and a very hush-hush secret tomato sauce passed through my lips and spurted in every direction. It coated the walls. It coated the glass of the shower doors in orange-red globs. It was a Dexter Morgan blood splatter. It was a Rorschach created by the devil himself. What didn't cascade onto my feet ricocheted off the porcelain and stuck to the hairs on my chest.

Suddenly I was standing in it. I was wearing it like an awards dress even Lady Gaga would shake her head and gawk at.

I tried to make it stop. I tried willing it to stop. *I failed.*

Sloppy, meaty chunks of steaming, partially digested mozzarella piled between my toes. They mixed with the spraying water and cascaded back against me. I was bathing in it.

Tears poured down my face. I covered my mouth with my hand in a desperate attempt to make it stop. This accomplished nothing. The devil puke squeezed through the spaces between my fingers. It would not be denied. It was the Terminator and Robocop and the Predator all mixed together. It was tougher then Lieutenant Marion "Cobra" Cobretti, and it wouldn't be stopped.

For nearly three minutes I continued to gag and spew, and stand in my toasty warm insides. When it was finally over, my legs gave way and I dropped to my knees in the steaming aftermath.

There was a knock at the door. "Steven? Are you okay?"

It was my wife: my goddamn wife, my late to the show wife.

"Steven?" I tried to tell her not to open the door. I tried to warn her, but a wad of half dissolved cheese the size of a testicle lodged in my throat made it impossible.

The instant she stepped into the bathroom the sickening acid odor hit her nose. It shot into her stomach, then back into her mouth and into her belly once again like a demonic game of pong. At some point during the journey the awful scent triggered her gag reflex. A moment later she was keeled over and hacking as well. Her hacking succeeded in furthering my own, and my hacking was doing the same to her.

She was useless to me. The whole thing was moronic. It was stupid.

Back and forth we traded gags and coughs, and belched with our eyes closed and our hands over our mouths. She kept insisting that she needed to help and I kept insisting that she get the hell out of the room.

The air smelled like unwashed ass, like the underside of Rachael's Ray's boobs after a sweat-drenched trip to the gym, or her recipe for Lasagna Florentine.

Unable to stand it any longer, my wife crawled from the bathroom and slammed the door behind her. I was happy to have her gone.

I spent the next twenty minutes cleaning up my own filth. I soaked my feet, popped open a bottle of body wash and dumped it onto my head. I lathered my legs and soaped my chest and scrubbed my various patches of cheese-sticky body hair. I scooped a piece of half-digested cheese from underneath my balls.

When my body had been fully sanitized, I went to work on the tub itself. I scrubbed the walls and the basin, all while trying my damnedest to keep Biff from getting riled up again.

When I returned to the bedroom, I dropped to the bed and closed my eyes.

My wife placed her hand on my shoulder. "Is there anything I can do to help?"

It took everything I had not to punch her in the tit.

The next morning she found a dried-up piece of stomach cheese on the bathroom floor that I'd somehow missed. She started hacking.

I felt a little bit better.

CRAZY FAMILY

CRAZY FAMILY

The last times I saw my Uncle Phil was when I was a senior in college. It was during an awkward visit to my father's. Someone had the bright idea to get a bonfire started in an empty field across from Phil's house. This, of course, brought out the neighborhood.

Bonfires attract hillbillies like bug zappers attract moths, only the hillbillies don't generally jump in and get killed. *Well, most of the time, anyway.*

In no time at all, Phil was chasing some of the local kids around with a stick that had a still flaming marshmallow on it and bellowing something mostly nonsensical about "roasted kid nuts."

Why was he doing this? *Hell if I know.* He was Phil, and bringing up the testicles of ten-year-old boys in conversation was the sort of stuff Phil did.

That's not a good enough answer for you? *Let me try to explain things further.*

First off, I suppose I should describe my uncle Phil to you. Phil's a huge guy. He's at least 6'4", and maybe even 6'5". The dude weighs in at around three hundred and fifty pounds, maybe more. A hundred or so of those pounds are carried in his gut alone. Phil's been in his third trimester for twenty-five years. While I'm anxiously awaiting the delivery, it disturbs the hell out of me to think about what exactly he's going to deliver. I'm imagining a weird mix of the girl from the movie *Precious* and old Chevy Chase.

Out of breath and gasping for air, Phil tossed the still flaming marshmallow into his mouth and began to stroll in my direction, his Chicago Bears parachute pants flapping in the breeze. Reaching down, he grabbed a handful of his shirt and pulled it over his baby mount. Pulled far past its limits, the material immediately popped back up. That thing simply could not be denied.

His voice was like drunken thunder. "Hey, turd!" He cracked me on the shoulder with a stiff right hook before his fists went to his face. "Damn it, kid! You get bigger every time I see you!" Suddenly he was throwing jabs at me like Rocky Marciano. No, wait, not Rocky Marciano — more like Rocky Marciano's elderly, smoke-riddled, overweight grandfather.

"You wanna go? Come on, turd! Let's see what you got in dem turd hands of yers!" He was plodding around me, his oversized meathooks resting just below his chin and his toothless maw grinning in my direction.

"Let's do this, turd! I'll have you shittin' yer britches before the second round!"

What?

Needless to say, I had no interest in "going." Luckily, Phil's attention was drawn away from me and back to the bonfire when some of the kids he was chasing earlier began screaming and jumping around like crazies. Apparently they'd stumbled onto a field mouse.

One of the connections in Phil's brain fired off. From his perspective, a mouse plus a fire equaled throw it in. Which is exactly what he did.

That's my uncle Phil in a nutshell. He's the very act of reaction. He's a moment in time. He's the culmination of this very first thought and nothing more and, well, he is who he is. He's an oversized beer swilling wacko, who never learned wrong from right, or simply doesn't give a crap — *maybe a little of both.*

While I would imagine that almost everyone has their own version of an Uncle Phil, I have the original. Trust me on this. They broke the mold when they made this guy. They broke it, pissed on it and tossed it into a volcano so it could never be copied.

At my father's wedding to my step-mother quite some years back, both Phil and his loving counterpart, Mrs. Phil, had to be locked in a camper in my father's backyard during the reception.

They were like a couple of drunken gorillas that needed to be hidden from the prying eyes of the visitors in order to keep them from snapping the bars of their cage and rampaging through the streets.

When the door to the camper closed behind them, oh, the sounds they made. You know that high-pitched wail cats sometimes make when they get on their hind legs and start to snarl? Imagine that noise. Now replace the cat with large pieces of farm equipment, double it, give it some guns, maybe a couple knives and a bazooka or two. Have a voodoo priestess fill these bizarre new concoctions with the spirits of long dead killers and slather it all in a tub of duck fat. *Honestly, I'm amazed that camper held them in check.*

Some years ago I received a phone call from my younger brother that went something like this:

"Hey Steve, did you hear about Dad?"

"No. Why? What happened?"

"He spent the weekend in jail."

"No kidding? What did he do?"

"Well, apparently he got into a fight with Phil and someone called the cops."

My brother went on to tell me that Phil made some sort of remark about my father's wife—called her a slut or something, I think—who knows? Anyway, my father tried to leave and Phil threw a beer bottle at the back of his head. It connected and this naturally led to a couple of old dudes wrestling on the front lawn. *Well, naturally in the case of these two, anyway.* The cops showed up and they ended up wrestling the cops. Everyone was arrested and everyone was thrown in jail.

It was a tale worthy of a Jerry Springer episode; you know, without anyone flashing their tits, unless you count Phil's. And I'm not counting Phil's, because just thinking about that makes me want to dip my face in sulfuric acid.

Believe it or not, there are people out there that doubt my seriousness when I tell them one of my goals in life was to end my bloodline. *Silly people.*

I hadn't heard from Phil in a very long time. Until suddenly, a couple of years ago, I received a birthday card completely out of the blue (especially since it was June and my birthday is in December). The card was from Phil and Mrs. Phil.

What the hell?

The guy had never sent me a birthday card before. This was a man who'd been fired from three jobs *(that I knew of)* for randomly punching a co-worker or boss in the face. Seriously, he just hauled off and clocked them, without a care in the world, and he did it more than once.

There is a not so fine line between "balls" and "stupidity," and Phil dropped a steamer on that line years ago.

I opened the card, and staring back at me in chicken scratch more akin to the handwriting of a kindergartner rather than that of a grown man were the words, *"Happy birthday, turd."*

The man's all class.

The thing that worried me then and still worries me today, and the thing I still can't figure out, is how the hell he managed to get my address in the first place.

I'm not too interested in brawling on my front lawn.

I'M THE VOICE OF REASON?

I'M THE VOICE OF REASON?

By the time I was 23, I was a father to a teenage boy — well, a stepfather anyway.

It still counts. Sort of.

Is that weird? I guess it is. Maybe a little. Then again, I'd seen and done a whole lot of weird up to that point, with weird rapidly becoming the norm. My life has always been *weird* and more than likely it'll remain that way.

While I might not have any idea how or when I'm going to die, I'm fairly positive it'll happen amidst confusing and/or humiliating circumstances. Can someone really be humiliated when they're dead, though? Eh, I'm sure I'll figure out how to pull it off.

Around the time I began my step-fatherly duties, my wife and my step-son had the exact relationship that pretty much every single teenage boy and his mother have at some point: an angry one.

Hell, I used to bitch and get into shouting arguments with my mother like you wouldn't imagine. We said things we didn't mean, screamed things we didn't want to scream, and made threats we had no intention of keeping. There were sentences uttered by the both of us that made even Don Rickles' most "blue" standup set pale in comparison.

NOTE TO SELF: Never bring up Don Rickles in a story again. If I keep doing that no one is ever going to believe that I'm under sixty-five with a fully functioning prostate.

The love/hate, hate/love, hate/hate relationship between mothers and their sons is a game as old as time. It's like greed and sex and William Shatner. It transcends race, has no interest in religion, and couldn't care less about social status. It's been going on since the first boy spit from the first vagina, and it won't stop happening anytime soon.

My wife and stepson could get into some real winners. They argued about girls. They complained about grades, and bitched about effort and moaned about work. They babbled about freedom and trust, and whined about stuff that happened in the past. They once even settled into an hour-long shouting match about the results of the Pepsi Challenge.

Or maybe I just made that up. Either way. *(Coke is the winner, by the way.)*

Honestly, I'm not entirely convinced that they ever knew exactly what they were fighting about. Want proof?

Let me hire some nefarious, gun toting Libyans to gun down Doc Brown in cold blood, hop into his time-traveling DeLorean, and take you back to one argument in particular.

My stepson had been having issues with his girlfriend at the time. He was in love and he was emotional, and he wasn't making much sense. My wife felt bad for him (as any mother would), but she wasn't sure how to help someone who clearly didn't want help. Because of this she was emotional as well, and because she was emotional she wasn't making much sense either. It was a perfect storm of idiocy, which, strangely, is the perfect way to describe the 1990's Helen Hunt action extravaganza, *Twister*.

"Fine then! Fine Mom! Is that what you want? Fine! I'll just leave then! I'll go live with my dad! I'll go live with him and I'll never come back! Is that what you want? Is it? Because it's what I'll do! I'll do it right now!"

"You don't want to go live with your father."

"Yes I do! I'll love it there! I'll go live with him right now! Then you'll never have to worry about me again!"

"Stop it!"

"No! I won't stop it! You stop it! You stop doing what you're doing and stop it! I don't have to stop anything!"

It was about 8:00 at night. The two of them were in the hallway outside Matt's bedroom. I was in the other room, reclined and comfortable and trying my damndest to enjoy an episode of The Simpsons. Their nonsensical ramblings were interfering with my television. I found this bothersome.

"Fine Matthew! Fine! You want to go live with your father? Fine! You've got to learn to deal with situations better! You can't just freak out all the time!"

"I'm not freaking out! You're freaking out! There's no way I'm freaking out! I'm not the freak here! You're the freak, Mom! You are!"

"Don't you dare call me that! Do you know what you do to me every time you act like this? Do you know how much it hurts me? Do you?"

The boy started huffing and the wife started crying.

I was a twenty-five-year-old man with the functioning brain of a twelve-year-old, but even I knew that it wasn't exactly in my best interest to butt my nose into the mother/son dynamic whenever things became heated. I wasn't his father. I was never going to be the kid's father, and to try and act like I was would have been silly. Plus I was just barely eight years older than him. I was more like an older brother, an older brother who had sex with his mother.

See? I told you my life was weird.

"Matthew? Wh-why, why do you do this to me? Can't you see how badly you treat me sometimes? I'm only trying to help! I'm only trying to be a mom and do the things moms are supposed to do out of love and caring and stuff, and tell you things that I know because I've been there, and I've learned them and I know them an—"

What?

"I don't need your help mom! I don't need anyone's help! I've got help! I've got lots of help and the help keeps coming from other places to offer me more of it! Everyone helps me all the time and I help myself even more!"

Huh?

They were babbling. Sense and reason had long since left the building. Sense opened up a flower shop in Toledo and reason was working on a screenplay while making ends meet as a barista at Jitter Beans in San Francisco.

The argument between my wife and stepson had quickly degraded into yelling for yelling's sake. They were screaming and crying, and babbling like a pair of lunatics sporting poop-stained pajamas in a mental ward. If Matt actually decided to actually leave the house and trek across town to his old man's, not only would they both end up regretting it, but I would be called on to console my wife for the next two hours while she cried on the bed.

I wasn't prepared to dedicate two more hours to this nonsense. I had more important thing to do, like pulling the wad of bunched up boxers from between my butt cheeks and continuing with The Simpsons. Homer had opened a Christian mission in a third world country and referred to Jesus as Jebus. *Jebus.* Come on, that's good stuff.

If there was ever a moment to ignore my longstanding neutral status and intervene, that moment had arrived. I stood with an annoyed huff, strutted to the hallway with my chest puffed, and stepped between them while looking buffed.

Actually I wasn't very buffed. *Rhyming is just fun.*

"Okay, that's enough. Why don't we all take a deep breath and calm down."

Surprisingly, they stopped yelling.

"I'm going to be perfectly honest with the both of you. Neither of you is making any sense, and I think that maybe you need to take a break from this. Go your separate ways, relax, chill out and you can come back to it later. I mean, seriously, this is absolutely the worst argument I've ever heard in my life and I consider myself to be dumber for having listened to it."

They didn't speak.

"Yeah, that's right, you've made me dumber. And I was pretty dumb to begin with…so soak on them apples."

I'm not sure what that last bit meant. I pretended I never said it, hoped they hadn't heard it, and returned to The Simpsons. Fifteen minutes later they hugged and made up.

By the time I was 23 I had a teenage stepson.

By the time I was 25 I had a vasectomy.

LIFE OF THE PARTY

LIFE OF THE PARTY

I'm not exactly the most personable guy you're ever going to meet. I'm just not. I haven't been in a very, very long time. My wife knew this about me when she met me in the seedy underbelly of online dating. She knew it when I nearly plotzed my pantaloons the first time I was introduced to her friends, and she certainly knew it when I actually did plotz my pantaloons the first time I was introduced to her family.

Just to be clear, I have absolutely no idea what "plotzed my pantaloons" means. *It makes me chuckle, though.*

My problem is that I freeze up when I'm around large groups of people. My muscles lock, my legs refuse to move, and the grilled cheese sandwich I had earlier in the day comes rushing into my throat on a river of bile and mashed up stomach glop. The same thing actually happens around small groups of people. And around more than two people. I can't help it.

Am I proud of it? *Of course not.* Is it something I'd put on a resume? *Depends on the job, I suppose.* Do I wish I could communicate with other human beings on a face-to-face basis without blitzing my britches? *Damn straight.* Am I happy that I replaced "plotzed my pantaloons" with "blitzed my britches?" *The jury's still out.*

Despite the fact that my wife has dealt with my bizarre, crippling social anxieties for years, she still somehow manages to seem surprised every time it happens. It's like the woman has Memento-memory, minus the tattoos and Christopher Nolan.

"What was up with you tonight, Steven?"

"Well, that was an odd performance."

"Why were you acting like that?"

"You didn't have to act like that. You could have mingled a bit, you know."

"You know, if you didn't want to come to the birthday party, you didn't have to."

GAH!

Honestly, I'm not sure what she's thinking. It's like she expects things to suddenly go differently every time, like she thinks a little light bulb will suddenly turn on in my brain and just like that, I'll be chugging back shooters and doing a jig on the table with the punch bowl at her friend's Christmas party.

I wish I could. I wish it were that simple. Unfortunately, it's not.

That being said, it might surprise you to learn that I don't particularly like disappointing my wife unless I'm disappointing her in the sack. Because of that I usually try my damndest to ignore my natural instincts and be a bit more personable on the rare occasions that she drags me from the shadows and into the sun.

For example, at a get-together a while back, I convinced myself that I was really going to put my best foot forward. I was sick of seeing the look of utter defeat in her eyes on the ride home. I wanted to make her proud. I wanted to leave a party for once and have her say something like, "Well done, Steven!" or "That jig you did near the punch bowl was incredible! Where did you learn to do that?"

I wanted to be able to point to my feet and say, "These bitches were just doing what came naturally." and flash her a pair of jazz hands.

For once in my life I was going to be the man she wanted me to be! I was going to wow her! I was going to take her breath away and moisten her lady area! I was going to make every woman jealous of her and every man momentarily consider going gay! I was going to put on a show! *It was go time, damn it!*

The moment we arrived, I peeled away from my sullen-faced gal and headed for a crowd. Accustomed to having me follow her awkwardly around the room like a remora clinging helplessly to a shark, this took my wife by surprise. "Steven, are yo—"

"I'm fine." I didn't even let her finish. There was no time for pleasantries. I was on a mission. I waved a hand in her general direction and stomped across the room like Leeroy Jenkins into the heat of battle with an ostrich leg in one hand and a battleaxe in the other.

Shit just got real.

I spotted some of the other husbands hanging out in the backyard. They were hovering around the grill flipping burgers with mustaches on their faces, bellies hanging over their belts, and beers in their hands. They weren't regulars. I didn't recognize any of them. So what? *Who cares? This was my chance.*

I didn't have a mustache, I didn't have a beer and I didn't want a mustache or a beer. *This was still my chance.*

I approached the herd of potbellied grazers with my chest puffed and my back straightened. I moved my hands from my pockets and placed them on my hips in a manner more befitting my manly, open, and anxious to chat nature. I replaced the scowl on my face with something coming slightly closer to a vague sort of smile.

"So listen to this…" When I arrived they were in already in the middle of a conversation. I nodded my head and tried to look interested. "After the game I pulled my kid's coach aside, and I put my finger right in that asshole's face. I told him that Scotty doesn't play third base. Scotty plays second base. And if I ever saw Scotty playing third base again, Scotty wouldn't be playing at all."

Hm.

The manly group of manly husbands nodded their head in agreement and took a swig of their bubbly elixirs.

Hm.

Another one of them chimed in, his mustache blowing in the breeze, freckled with specks of hot dog bun, and raccoon, and pig hoofs, and diced eel wang, and leather boot, and whatever the hell they make hot dogs out of. "I had the same problem with Brit's piano teacher. The woman didn't think Brit was ready for a recital, and I was like, you know what, I'm pretty sure I know when my kid is ready for a recital. I'm not paying you to tell me what to do. This is America, lady. I don't know how they do it back in communist Taiwan, or whatever, but that's not how it works here."

"Fucking-A."

"I was like, you take my money? You do what I say. End of story."

"Yep. I heard that."

Hm.

Despite its obvious flaws this seemed to make perfect sense to everyone.

Hm.

The discussion eventually turned to work.

"Ug. Don't even get me started. Do you have any idea how many idiots I have to deal with on a daily basis? Brainless morons, every last one of them is a clown. One after another. It's a conveyor belt of dummies. I swear, half the human race hasn't evolved from the caveman days."

"And half of those out of work bastards actually believe in that shit."

"What shit?"

"Evolution."

"Yeah, no kidding. God damn liberals."

Hm.

And then there was politics. "We should have killed that Obama when we had the chance."

Hm.

And food. "Speaking of Obama, looks like I burnt the burgers."

Ug.

And drugs. "If I ever found out that Alex was smoking pot on the weekends, his ass hits the street."

Sigh.

After listening and smiling blindly for ten minutes, I'd had enough. I'd picked a really bad group of guys to begin my great "personable Steve" experiment. My plan had failed miserably. *This just wasn't going to work.*

I was about to walk away when my new friends decided to bring me into their Ku Klux Konversation. "Hey, Steven. Did that book of yours come out?"

I wasn't sure how they knew my name and I sort of hoped they would forget it.

"Yeah."

"How's it selling?"

Shrug.

This was followed by an awkward silence, and that awkward silence was immediately followed by another awkward silence. There might have even been a third awkward silence.

Sick of staring at me blanking and occasionally sipping their beers, my new pals eventually returned to chatting amongst themselves and I shuffled away shaking my head. *For once my unresponsiveness had paid off.*

I never got around to dancing on the table with the punch bowl, which is probably for the best. I'm a terrible dancer.

-Steven Novak-

ME VS. BABY: WINNER TAKES ALL

ME VS. BABY: WINNER TAKE ALL

I hate kids. Okay, maybe *hate* isn't exactly the correct term. I shouldn't say that I *hate* them. I'm just completely disgusted by them, and the poop in their pants, and their goo-covered fingers, and their bizarre, crooked, no-toothed grins.

If by chance we ever meet, and you happen to bring your kid along, don't be upset if I show very little interest at all in it. Don't take it personally. It's not that I think your kid in particular is gross as much as I think all kids are gross. There's a reason I paid a doctor to take a scalpel to my nuts up in my early twenties and it sure as hell wasn't because I adore tiny, useless bags of *chubandspitandcrap*.

On the off chance that you find my dislike of wide-eyed, foul smelling, sticky-fingered human beings confusing, let me take this opportunity to at least explain myself.

One day my wife and I stopped by her aunt's house briefly to say hello and get a good look at the new addition to the family.

"The baby's here! Come over and see the baby!"

"Ohmygawd the baby will be here for a few hours! Hurry up and come look!"

"Baby! Come see the baby! Come see now!"

"Holy Shit You've Gotta See This Motherfucking Baby!"

These are the kind of phone calls my wife gets on a regular basis, and believe it or not, she's actually excited when she gets them.

Personally, I don't get it.

The kid doesn't walk. The kid can't talk. The kid can't sing me a song, or tell me a story. It can't chat with me about comics, or music, or make useless small talk about the weather, or pretend to be interested in any of the mostly pointless nonsense that spews from my mouth. The kid can't really do anything other than poop. It can poop and it can drool, and when it's done doing that it can poop and drool some more, right on top of the previous poop and drool.

Maybe I am missing something, or maybe my soul is too black and my brain too jaded, but babies in general seem pretty damn useless. I don't know.

I guess it's just me. It has to be, right? Why else would there be so many people on the planet—you know, other than the fact that people really like sex and really hate to cover their dongs in latex.

Even if it is, that doesn't necessarily make me wrong. *Call me when you can help me with my taxes at the end of the year. Until then, good luck with that whole diarrhea diaper thing.*

Anyway, I was sitting on the couch next to my wife's cousin, who was also the father of the little bundle of joy, and he had the squirming, fleshy creep show in his arms. Did I forget to mention that he'd just announced to the room that the kid had, in fact, shit her britches?

Wonderful.

With this bit of knowledge in my head, I noticed that the baby was looking right at me. She was staring at me with a peculiar sort of smile on her face. She was looking me over and scanning me for weaknesses. The little jerk was planning something. Something flashed behind those dead blue eyes: inspiration, maybe, undoubtedly nefarious in nature.

She knew exactly what she was going to do. She knew that the shimmery dollop of slobber on her mouth and the bulge of compacted crap ballooning her diaper was freaking me out. *Oh yeah, she knew.*

With a bubbly, baby food smelling gurgle, she began crawling toward me. In no time at all the horizontal crawl turned vertical. Suddenly she was climbing up me. Within seconds she was a mere three inches from my face, leaning wobbly on my shoulder on her stubby legs. Her blank eyes latched onto mine. Her mouth opened and a river of spittle rolled over her chin. Her soaked lips curled into a crooked smile. Her expression was undeniable. Without ever saying a word she was telling me, *"I've got you now, you uncomfortable pathetic loser."*

And she was right.

The river of mucus drool was hanging perilously from her chin, swaying back and forth as she wobbled on uneven legs and glistening in the light from the window behind us. I had to get rid of it. I needed it removed from my field of vision before my brain exploded inside my skull.

Breathing heavily, I snagged the sleeve of her little baby suit and used it to wipe her face clean. "You um, you got a little something there, don't ya? Yeah, let me help you out with that."

Mission accomplished.

While I felt slightly less queasy, the poop remained, encased in her diaper and smeared against her baby-soft butt cheeks. I could smell it. It was pungent and it was foul and it was permeating the air. A crash, or a call, or something drew the attention of her father for the moment. My mind was too preoccupied with the bouncing bag of crab dangling from my shoulder to know for sure.

He stood from the couch. "Crap. Can you watch her for a minute?"

I wanted to grab him by the wrist, toss him to the floor and kick him square in the scones! What was he thinking? I wanted to watch his kid about as much as I wanted to sit though a weekend long retrospective of the collected films of Michael Bay!

The kid's hand moved unexpected to my face and I froze. She was pawing at my cheek and poking me in the eye with the tips of her sticky fingers. *The balls on this kid! The unmitigated gall!*

She was blatantly invading my personal space! She was touching and slapping and looking me right in the eyes and doing it with a devilish grin so devilish that Beelzebub himself would have blushed. *The nerve! The absolute moxie!*

I was moments from screaming when her father returned to the couch, scooped her up and pulled her away. He tossed her over his shoulder and carried her to the next room to clean the feces from her flesh. She was smiling at me the entire time. While I can't be sure, I think she might have even given me the finger. *The audacity.*

I don't *get* babies. I never have and I never will. I don't understand the allure. They are essentially human beings who mumble, cry and crap their own pants. I don't even particularly care for human beings that don't do any of that stuff.

You know what they call homeless guys on the street who do the same thing? They call them crazy people. As a society we've made it a point to catch crazy people and toss them into mental institutions, and deservedly so.

It should never be acceptable for human beings of any age to stew in their own still-warm feces, even if they happen to be involved in some sort of feces-stewing competition or something.

Speaking of which, if such a thing exists, it really shouldn't.

Please don't let it exist.

-Steven Novak-

**EIGHT MINUTES.
NOWHERE NEAR NINE.**

EIGHT MINUTES. NOWHERE NEAR NINE.

The weekend in Vegas was coming to an end. We had dinner, we had sex, and we walked the strip and briefly considered taking in a *risqué* topless show before giggling like preteen idiots and scampering away.

We also did the one and only thing I dragged my wife to Vegas for in the first place: spend hour upon hour at the Star Trek Experience exhibit in the Hilton. *And yes, in case you were wondering, it was better than the sex.*

At the Experience I read through the comprehensive timeline retelling the history of the Star Trek universe. I rode not only the Next Generation simulator ride, but the Borg Encounter one as well. I paid insane amounts of money for memorabilia that included an original series Science Officer shirt, A Ferengi statue, and no less than five books filled with detailed episode retellings from each and every series. I paid even more money to have a piece of lemon chicken served to me by a guy in full Klingon make-up.

Long story short, it was a perfect weekend.

Sure, money was spent — a lot of money — but I got something substantial and real for each and every dime pulled from my pocket. Granted, maybe the things I purchased aren't something that you necessarily have an interest in, or even understand. Maybe you're not the kind of person that thinks a black baseball jersey with the word Klingons on it is cool. That's your prerogative. My purchases might have been dorky, and nerdy, and at times fairly fucking lame, but they were tangible. My money was exchanged for goods and services. There is no arguing this fact.

My wife on the other hand, well, she went a different route.

Oh, by the way, before I continue, let me just say that if you don't think a Klingon baseball jersey is cool, well, you and I are just never going to see eye to eye. *Damn no-taste weirdo.*

The wife and I were in the elevator, on our way to check out and make the drive back through the desert to home, when she turned to me and said, "Give me some money. I want to gamble for a bit while you take the bags out to the car."

A lump the size of an engorged pair of testicles formed in my throat. "Are you sure? I thought you said you weren't going to gamble this weekend?"

"Come on, Steven. Just give me whatever you've got left in your wallet. We're about to leave. How can I go to Las Vegas and not gamble even once?"

I knew it was a bad idea the minute she said it, but what could I do? She was an adult and she wasn't an idiot—most of the time, anyway. She was of sound mind and body, and technically half of the money in my pocket was hers to being with. Plus, as much as I hated to admit it, she sort of had a point. How much damage could she do in the time it would take me to walk to the car, put the bags in the trunk, and walk back?

I dug into my wallet, pulled out a *hundy* and slapped it into her open palm.

Quick note: Did you happen to notice that I just typed the word "hundy" instead of "hundred?"

What the hell? Where do I get off doing something like that? Who do I think I am? I'm not the sort of guy that can pull off "hundy." I'd have better luck pulling off a triple sow cow and finishing with a quadruple horse pie, which isn't even a thing.

When the elevator door opened, my wife went one way and I went the other. I checked out, made my way through the revolving door, across the street and into the parking structure across the street.

I had a kick ass spot. I mean, I don't usually like to brag, but holy crapburger that was a sweet parking spot. It was as sweet like butterscotch vagina, which strangely smells atrocious, but even more strangely tastes delicious.

I threw the bags in the trunk, took a moment to inhale the desert air, and started back. I walked back across the street, through the revolving door, and headed toward the casino. The entire trip took me no more than seven minutes — maybe eight, but nowhere near nine.

As I entered the casino my wife shuffled toward me with her shoulders drooped and her head pointed to the floor.

Keep in mind the words *Eight minutes, nowhere near nine*. She couldn't have been done already. *Could she?*

"Sick of gambling already?"

She looked up at me and nodded, then lowered her head again.

"How much money do you have left?"

She didn't answer. Instead she slid past me and began heading for the exit.

No way. I caught up to her quickly. "Hey. Hello? How much money do you have left?"

Never once breaking stride, with her back to me she mumbled the word, "None."

The broad had lost one hundred dollars. She burned through the *hundy* like it was a witch in Salem. She tore through that Benjamin like my ass through my pants when I gained a bunch of weight in 2008. She did it all in eight minutes, nowhere near nine.

That's got to be some sort of pathetic Vegas record, right? I really need to contact those fine folks at Guinness.

CONVERSATION AT THE HEAD TABLE

CONVERSATION AT THE HEAD TABLE

A while back my little brother said goodbye to the carefree life of a single man and married himself a lady. To say I was happy for him would be a massive understatement.

Despite being well aware of my complete and total lack of even the most basic in social graces, he wanted me to be his best man and he wanted me to make a toast at the reception in honor of the occasion. To say I was terrified of this would be an even more massive understatement than the previous massive understatement.

In the end, my toast ended up sucking fairly hard. It sucked as hard as a supercharged suck machine with realistic lips and über-sucking ability made to look like *Xena: Warrior Princess* and created by a lonely nerd for the sole purpose of suckling his nerdy "lightsaber."

Depending on who you ask, it might have sucked even harder than that. I managed to work a reference to a white rhino into it somehow. I really did that.
I shit you not.

This story isn't really about my piss-poor toasting abilities, however. It's actually about some of the conversation going on at the head table during the dinner.

Here are a few examples of topics covered:

"If everyone in the wedding party suddenly started fighting—no weapons, just fists—who do you think would win?"

"Did'ya hear that Mr. T is getting his own show? I pity 'da channel 'dat gives T his own show!"

"Do you think you'd be able to beat up your father in a fight—no weapons, just fists? You know, if you were forced to go at it bare-knuckled in a crazy space arena or something?"

"How many of the servers do you think are gay?"

"One of us should ask them if they're gay, otherwise how are we gonna know if we're right?"

"Will and Grace was, without a doubt, the dumbest show on television, wasn't it?"

"Which fork is for the salad?"

"When are they serving the salad?"

"Can I skip the salad?"

"I'll pay you fifty dollars right now if you go onto the middle of the dance floor, drop your pants and take a dump. Then you have to pull them up and come sit back like nothing happened."

"If you act like something happened and make a big deal about it you only get twenty-five."

This was all before drinks had even been served. That means the age-old "I was drunk and I didn't know what I was saying" excuse wasn't going to fly in this case.

And they say the art of intelligent conversation is dead.

The discussion really got interesting when the topic of women and their oh-so-wonderful womanly parts made its first appearance. "Oh yeah, what about that one? Would you hit that?" That was my brother's friend, Jason. Jason was sitting beside me at the head table and motioning toward a rather busty woman in a strapless dress on the opposite end of the reception hall.

"She's alright. She's not really my style, but yeah, I'd give it to her good."

That was, Scotty, another of my brother's friends and one of the last men in America to think a mustache was an acceptable choice for facial hair. Scotty was sitting beside Jason and trying his damndest to pretend the girl in the strapless dress wasn't "his style." You know, because chesty blonde women with legs that don't quit are often turned away when it comes to the bedroom. *Scotty wasn't fooling anyone.*

Pretty much everyone in the wedding party, myself included, was comprised of two parts nerdiness, one part dorkocity, and one part loserdom. Each of us had been beaten with the ugly stick at some point in our lives before being shoved into the oven and cooked at three-fifty for forty-five minutes.

The idea that any of us had a "style" was as crazy as Little Cesar's patented Crazy Sauce recipe.

"What about her?"

"Who, the red-haired girl?"

"No, the one next to her."

"What? She's old enough to be my mom."

"So, she's still pretty hot. I'd knock her womb around a bit."

I wasn't a part of the conversation, but I started laughing. I admit it. The "knocking of the womb" thing was funny. Plus, nerds talking sex makes me laugh. Why? Because nerds know nothing about sex.

That's part of the reason we're nerds. And it's because we know so very little about sex that we really shouldn't be allowed to talk about sex. We just end up sounding stupid. This is the same reason Katy Perry really shouldn't ever say anything about anything. Other than maybe "Look at my boobs jiggle."

Jason heard me laughing and said, "What about you Steve, would you knock around that girl's chicken box?"

Chicken box? What the hell? *I'm not even going to begin to try and figure that one out.*

Until this point I hadn't really said much over the course of the evening. I'm not much of a talker. I'm more of a listener, I guess. I listen and I take a lot of notes for stories to write in books at some point down the line.

It was at this moment that I decided to take the conversation to a whole other level. I needed to remind those nerdy jokers of why I didn't talk much and maybe disgust and scare them a little bit in the process. Basically, I was bored.

"Naw, that's a chicken box you don't want to go digging in. I'll tell you who I would hit though…that one, right over there."

Jason and Scotty followed the creepy motioning of my head and looked toward the back of the room. When they didn't spot anything even coming close to an attractive woman they were noticeably confused. "Wait, where? Who are you talking about?"

"Right there. The one wearing red."

"Who? Where?"

"With the red top."

They still had no idea who the hell I was talking about. Scotty scratched his head. Jason stood in order to get a better look and still saw nothing.

"Who the hell are you—" Suddenly, as if Anderson Silva blasted him in the face in the third round of a UFC Middleweight title fight, Jason realized who I was talking about. He swallowed. "The little boy?"

There was little boy in a red button-up shirt across the room. He was wiping snot from his nose and picking at the seat of his poop-filled pants.

"Yep. You better believe it."

I played it serious. I kept a totally straight face, gave my lips a little lick and allowed by brief glance to transform into a lusty, "this guy needs to be in prison" sort of stare. I don't think they actually thought I was serious – at least I hope not.

It was a terrible joke made by a bored man who was disappointed with his piss poor toast earlier in the evening, and a poor sense of humor to boot.

Neither Scotty nor Jason talked to me for the rest of the night. So I guess something good came from it.

LEPRECHAUN PERVERTS AND LADY POKING

LEPRECHAUN PERVERTS AND LADY POKING

It started out like any other Tuesday morning—and by that I mean, like shit.

The alarm clock went off at 7:00 and my half asleep, half awake, half pissed off ass crawled out of bed and stumbled like a rum-soaked, Karloff-legged mummy to the bathroom. And yes, before you say anything, I am fully aware that the universal concepts of math make the idea of three halves impossible. My response is simple: *fuck you*. At 7:00 in the morning two plus two can equal fifty-forty, eight minus nine can equal plurdteen and Dane Cook can be the funniest comic in the history of stand-up for all I care.

At 7:00 in the morning the impossible becomes possible, and until my bladder is emptied, the possible becomes the truth.

When I entered the bathroom I clicked on the light, looked into the mirror and nearly dropped a shockload into my Spiderman boxers. *Oh crap*.

My chest, face, and legs were covered in peanut-shaped, light-pink spots. I pulled out the waistband of my boxers and checked on my little buddy. For the most part he seemed okay. Unfortunately the area surrounding him was covered in the splotchy red weirdness as well. *Oh poop*.

When I went to bed the night before I looked perfectly normal, and I woke up resembling a male version of little orphan Annie. *Oh sheet*.

I returned to the bedroom and nudged my wife. When she didn't move my nudge transformed into a shove and I nearly rolled her off the bed. This got her attention.

"Is it just me, or am I covered in spots?"

Half-awake, half-asleep, and half-annoyed, she reluctantly crawled out of bed and asked me to step into the light of the bathroom to confirm what I was seeing. Her index finger reached forward and poked me in the chest. "Yeah. Yeah, it looks like you are."

When she was done poking me, she poked me again. Her eyes narrowed and her nose scrunched. I swear she looked like she was examining some sort of weird half-dead hobo corpse she stumbled onto in an alley. "You know what Steven, we should take you to the emergency room."

Emergency room? I didn't like the sound of that. I'm not a huge fan of doctors and I'm even less a fan of the word emergency.

"You think? I don't know…"

"Steven, come on. This isn't normal. You need to have it looked at."

Her lips curled and she started poking me again. A part of me expected her to disappear into the other room and return wearing one of those giant white suits with the gas masks for the face. You know, the ones those sons of bitches that killed E.T. wore.

Damn E.T. killing assholes! Why could you see that the little bastard just wanted to get home!

I insisted on taking an extremely quick shower and then called work to tell them I was heading to the *emergency room*. Fifteen minutes later we were there. An hour after that I was sitting on one of those annoying crunchy, paper-covered tables with my shirt off, while the doctor examined the spots on my chest much the way my wife had earlier. Under normal circumstances I think it might have been sort of hot to have two women poking at me while shirtless before 9:00 in the morning. Unfortunately these weren't normal circumstances. Plus they were both fully dressed at the time, and seemed a bit grossed out by me, and had no interest in pleasuring my genitals.

I really wish more women had interest in pleasuring my genitals.

Actually, I found myself fighting the urge to pop both of my poke-happy ladies in their respective jaws and let them discover what teeth taste like when they're rolling around in your mouth.

The doctor's eyes narrowed a bit behind her glasses. She shook her head and sighed. "Hm. Give me a second. I'll be right back."

She returned a few minutes later and shot me up with something while explaining that I was having an allergic reaction to the penicillin I'd been given the day before. This was strange, because until that very moment I'd never been allergic to penicillin.

In my head, I blamed my wife. I'm not sure why. Maybe it was because I was pissed off about the entire situation, or maybe it was because of her shifty, shifty eyes. *She knows she has shifty eyes. I'm not saying anything she doesn't already know.*

The doctor left the room again, but not before telling me that I needed to remain where I was for fifteen or so minutes so they could monitor me. The moment she was gone some pretty white clouds fluffed to life on the interior walls of my eyes. The world turned wobbly. The walls bent like a droopy wiener and the floor wrinkled like a chilly nutsack. My breaths felt deeper. They were more airy. A clown danced into the room, attached a tube to my head, and began to fill my brain with helium. It tickled.

Within minutes I was swaying back and forth like a doped-up slacker at a Phish concert. A crooked smile stretched itself across my face. If I'd known any Peter Paul and Mary songs, I might have started to sing them. Apparently, whatever the doc shot me up with was taking effect.

I was feeling good. I was feeling really good and I was enjoying it. I felt so good that if a three hundred and fifty pound guy calling himself "Stabber" would have raped me on the floor like a bitch lifer in a prison shower, I might have been okay with it. Hell, I might have even enjoyed it.

Suddenly nothing mattered. Suddenly everything was pretty. Suddenly even my wife's eyes didn't seem so shifty.

After another fifteen minutes the ladyDoc told my wife it was okay to take me home. She also gave us a prescription, which we decided to drop off at the Walgreens a block away.

When we pulled into the parking lot, my wife tried to convince me that I needed to wait in the car. I insisted that I go in. I really wanted to step outside and get a look at all the pretty new colors in the sky. I also wanted to figure out if there really was a unicorn on fire darting in and out of the clouds.

Poor stupid unicorn. I bet a leprechaun lit him up. *Leprechauns are jerks.*

The girl at the prescription counter took my information and started typing something in the computer. I thought this was hilarious. She stopped for a minute and looked at me like I was from another planet, or one of those creepy thirty-five-year-old, mother-of-three Twilight fans with Bella tattooed on one arm and Edward on the other.

"Is he okay?"

I'm not sure why, but I also found her question hilarious. In my drugged-addled state the prescription woman seemed as funny as

Louis C.K. She was cracking me up. In no time at all I was laughing and I was laughing loudly. Not only that, but I couldn't stop.

It was getting out of hand and it was more than a little weird. The prescription lady was getting uncomfortable. My laughter was like flying a kite at night, or eating a bowl of Captain Crunch with soymilk. It was unnatural and it was gross.

Laughter on the level of the laughter pouring from my mouth hadn't been heard since Charles Nelson Riley and Bret Butler were regulars on Match Game. *Or, wait. No. Maybe that wasn't the best example.*

Once our business with the girl behind the counter was done, my wife dragged her chuckling idiot of a husband from the store by his arm and shoved him into the car.

The flaming unicorn was gone from the sky. The leprechauns were roasting him over a fire in the parking lot of the Target across the way. *Damn leprechaun assholes.*

On the way home I looked at my wife and playfully nudged her shoulder. "Hey you."

"Hey what?"

I nudged her again, smacked my lips, and rolled my tongue across them awkwardly. "You know what? When we get home, we should totally screw. Howzabout it? Wanna screw?"

She looked at my peanut-spotted skin and my faraway stare and the drool dripping off my chin, and rolled her eyes. I have a feeling a part of her wished that she'd just let me go to work, even if it meant me dying.

When she didn't screw me, I screwed the leprechauns instead. *Leprechauns are such perverts.*

NEVER LET YOUR LADY SEE YOU WRESTLE

NEVER LET YOUR LADY SEE YOU WRESTLE

It's embarrassing to admit, but there was a time in my life when I actually missed backyard wrestling. I really did.

I'd moved from Illinois to California to be with my wife, and every once in a while I would get video tapes from my brother that featured him and his friends performing half-assed suplexes and bodyslams in my mother's basement, and it made me weep.

You see, I was a backyard wrestler for years, back when "backyard wrestling" was still new and hip and cool. Wait, maybe I shouldn't have included the words hip and cool.

New can stay, though.

It made me nostalgic to see my wrestling buddies carrying on without me. Don't get me wrong, I wasn't brought to the point of tears or anything, at least not that I'd admit.

I wanted to wrestle again. I wanted to film stupid little story lines, and throw someone around on a mattress, and get hit with cookie sheets, and hurt myself when I fell awkwardly. I wanted to make a complete ass out of myself and act a fool. The problem was that I had no friends.

Plus, even if I managed to scrape together a few pals during my first year or so in California, they would likely have been my own age and therefore had far more important things to do with their time: *you know, grown-ass adult things.*

Sounds crazy, right? I mean, what's more important than backyard wrestling? *cough-prettymucheverythingintheworld-cough*

There was one able body in the vicinity, however. There was one person I had a chance of convincing to join me in some backyard wrestling hijinks. That one person was my stepson, Matty.

Believe it or not, Matt is only eight years younger than I am, which makes him closer in age to me than I am to my wife.

I'm fully aware of the fact that it sounds a wee bit weird when you sit back and think about it, but it's always seemed to work for us, so bite me, Judgementaly Judgementalson.

Matty was instantly enthusiastic about the idea, and for the next three years or so, the two of us slapped on cheap Halloween masks once or twice a month, created stupid characters, and played out even stupider storylines while tossing each other around on a filthy mattress in my garage. It was a blast. And in a strange, bizzaro-land sort of a way, it proved to be a heck of an icebreaker when it came to the rather unique relationship we'd found ourselves in.

"If you ever really want to get to know someone just give them a DDT" – *Jake "The Snake" Roberts*

"If you ever want to ruin your career and end up snorting hash under a bridge in Akron, Ohio, give your opponents a DDT for fifteen years." – *Jake "The Snake" Roberts*

As fun as wrestling was and as good a time as we had doing it, on one occasion it came back to bite Matty right in the ass.

It was his fault. In a moment of haste, he broke the cardinal rule of backyard wrestling. The kid ripped to shreds the single rule a young man of any age never, ever wants to break when it comes to something like fake wrestling in your filthy garage. Matty did what he shouldn't have done, and in the end it not only hurt him, but his penis as well.

No one wants to hurt a penis, right? Well, unless it's hurt from too much sex? *I suppose that sort of hurt would be acceptable.*

I had just finished giving Matty a phenomenal belly-to-belly suplex and was fairly proud of myself when I heard the doorbell ring.

"Hey, Matt, did you hear that?"

He stood up and looked at me while trying to breathe through a particularly constricting mask. "What?"

"Did you hear something? I thought I heard the doorbell."

DING-DONG-DOONG

(That was my best impression of our doorbell. I'm pretty proud of it.)

Before I could even get a word out, Matty yelled, "I'll get it" and headed for the door.

He tore off his mask and had one foot into the house when I stopped him. "No. Just leave it. Don't worry about it."

Foolishly, he seemed intent on answering. "No. I'll get it."

The kid's hair was dripping wet and wilder than the famously wild mane of Doc Brown. He was covered in sweat. His shirt was drenched, and his pants were sopping. He smelled like the locker room at a teenage weight loss camp. Actually, he smelled more like the locker room at a teenage weight loss camp that's also filled with cat poop, because we kept the cat litter box in the garage.

Why anyone, anywhere, would want to greet strangers looking like he did at that moment, was beyond my level of understanding. Hell, maybe all of human understanding in general, and yet, the door closed behind him and in a puff of cartoonish smoke the kid was gone.

I stood alone in the garage for about five to ten minutes, all the while trying my damnedest to hear what was being said outside. After another couple of minutes, Matt shuffled back into the garage.

"Who was it?"

"What?" He was trying to avoid the question. He slipped his mask back on and indicated that he just wanted to get back to wrestling. I couldn't let him off that easily.

"Who was it?"

The kid sighed and lowered his head. It was a shameful pose. It was a pose I'd made myself more times than I could have possibly counted over the course of my life. I knew it well.

"It was just this girl, April, from work." *Ouch.*

Somehow he sighed even deeper. "She just wanted to say…I dunno…hello…I guess." *Ouch. Ouch. Double ouch with a kick square in the scones.*

"Is this the April that you've been talking to lately?"

"Yeah."

"Did she know what we were doing in here?"

"No."

"Did you tell her?"

"Not really. Sorta. I guess." *Eek.*

At this point I figured I should just stop asking questions. The poor bastard had suffered enough.

The next time Matty hit me with a cookie sheet it was harder than usual, and the next day the girl decided they weren't quite right for each other. *Eekity, ouch-ouch-eek, followed by a good old-fashioned painface.*

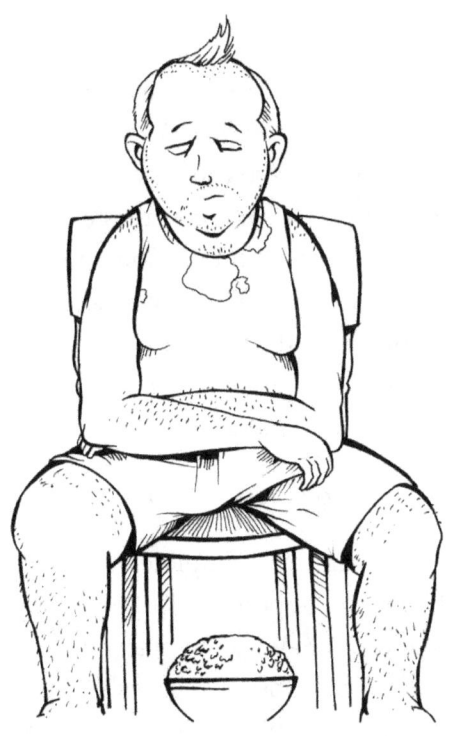

EVEN MY DREAMS SUCK

EVEN MY DREAMS SUCK

I dream a lot. Do I dream more than average Joe Average from somewhere in the middle of Average, Wisconsin? I dunno. I do dream a lot, though. In this case I want you to picture the words "a lot" like an enormous neon green and orange sign covered in fireworks, bright purple lights and random explosions that seem to be coming from nowhere at all. Then I want you to picture them hanging from the bottom of the Spruce Goose, covered in splattered birds and the corpses of Hollywood starlets as it somehow pulls off a mostly impossible figure eight at the world's largest air show.

So basically what I'm trying to say is that I dream a super-lot.

Sometimes my dreams are completely random and nonsensical and sometimes they feel like pompous little art house flicks that no one really understands, yet everyone pretends to. Most of the time though, my dreams come across like grossly over-the-top, big budget, summer Hollywood blockbusters. They're elaborate and glossy, and cheesy and saturated, and filled with dialog so idiotic you'd think it was written by a chimpanzee or possibly George Lucas.

I've been a secret agent. I've saved the world. I've been to distant planets and faraway lands. I've gone up against the mob and single-handedly taken down crooked cops. I've kicked a Hobbit in his nuts. I've given William Riker a wedgie and sensually peeled away Deanna Troi's form-fitting uniform. I've put God in a headlock and made him cry uncle. I've punched the devil in her vagina and I've even gone toe-to-toe with the American Ninja himself, Michael Dudikoff.

Note: Anyone who actually gets the Michael Dudikoff reference – *well, I feel sorry for you.*

Don't go thinking that all I do is smack around action heroes and saviors in my dreams, oh no, I also get laid - a lot. When I say a lot I mea—

Sigh. You know what? Let's not do that again.

I will say that dream Steve has dropped his britches and dove junk first into more lady parts than Wilt Chamberlin, Colin Farrell and John Holmes combined. White, Black, Mexican, Asian, Indian, Canadian, alien, cartoon, I've been with them all, sometimes three at once, and they all left satisfied. Trust me when I tell you that you haven't lived until you've been involved in a five-way with Salma Hayek, Joey Heatherton, Soleil Moon Frye, and the whirling gears of Arcee, who was in fact the most prominent of the female Autobots.

I almost forgot about Bugs Bunny in drag. *He/she was there too.*

With all these dreams and all the weird stuff going on in them, you'd think it would be difficult for me to be surprised by something. *Well, you'd think wrong.*

You see, a while back I had a dream that I haven't been able to get out of my head since. It was kind of hot, and sort of disturbing, and whole lot sad, with a Hindenburg-like load of *"oh, the humanity"* exploded on top. It has stuck with me ever since.

The bonkers dream in question began with me at the grocery store. I was in the frozen food aisle when a thick-mustached, blue-suit-wearing creep approached and told me that he was a director: a porno director.

The mustache should have been a dead giveaway.

Mustache McSexPeople asked if I'd be interested in becoming the star of his next flick. He claimed I had a "juicy look" about me, and that I was "oozing sexuality from every pore." He also claimed that he'd like nothing more than to see "sexy, sexy liquids dripping from the lens of a camera." Ignoring the fact that his sales pitch made me burp hot bile, it was an opportunity I couldn't pass up.

This of course cued a montage of me getting it on with sexy lady after sexy lady, winning various awards for my in-bed performances, and satisfying more women than every single vibrator in every single panty drawer of all the housewives in the world.

And of course, all of it was set to the 70's hit "Bang a Gong" by T.Rex. I kid you not, my friends. This song actually appeared in my dream. *That's right, I'm practically Shaft.*

Eventually I moved from in front of the camera to behind. I was doing double-duty, directing movies I didn't act in and acting in movies I was directing. I was working behind the camera. I was giving advice on hip movement and nipple tweaks. I was writing and I was making cameos just to keep my fans happy.

I know what you're thinking. *"Hey Steve, I've gotta tell you, I'm not sure what you're bitching about. This dream is the beez kneez, brotha!"*

Yes, it was indeed the beez kneez, brotha. No bones about it. *At least it was, up to that point.*

It was at this point that the dream fast-forwarded about ten or so. I'm older. I was more wrinkled, and I was still trying to make a buck in the porn business. Unfortunately, my star had begun to fade. Before my scenes I would sometimes find myself alone in the bathroom pumping away at my unresponsive, floppy ol' meathog, trying my damnedest to get the thing's attention and failing miserably. For reasons I can't fully explain, I was wearing white moccasins, an ivory loincloth, and there were feathers in my hair. *Maybe it was a Thanksgiving porno?* Oh, and on the loincloth, written in shimmering rhinestones were the words "disco fuck." *Maybe it was a 1970's Thanksgiving porno?*

The voice of the director chirped in from the other side of the bathroom door. "You almost ready in there, big guy? We need to shoot this."

"Just gimme ten minutes."

"We kinda need to shoot it now, honker. If you aren't up for it we ca—"

"Damn it! Can you just give me ten damn minutes?"

I slapped my manhood against the bathroom counter angrily. It sounded like a dead fish hitting a brick wall.

I pointed my finger at it and screamed, "Damn it! Why are you doing this to me, you son of a bitch? Get hard, you bastard! Do it! Do it now or I swear you'll regret it! You owe it to me! You owe me for everything I've done for you over the years!"

Needless to say, my penis didn't respond.

The dream fast-forwarded yet again. Suddenly it was fifteen years later. I was even older and my skin was more wrinkled than not. I was sporting a Fred Mertz-esque bald spot on my head, and I was broke. I was depressed, I was down, and I was still trying to scrape together the most meager of livings in the porn business.

I also seemed to be involved in some sort of weird "watch a gross, wrinkly, creepy old dude masturbate into a bowl of oatmeal" porn fetish.

There can't be a huge market for that, can there?

There I was, a seventy-plus-year-old man in a darkened room with a bowl of cinnamon flavor Quaker Oats on the floor that I was attempting to masturbate into while crying.

It was at this point that I woke up.

My wife woke up at almost the exact moment, rolled over to give me a morning smooch, and noticed a mixed bag expression on my face.

"Are you okay, Steven?"

"Yeah. Yeah, I'm fine. I just had a weird dream."

"About what?"

"It was a sex dream."

"Really?" Suddenly she was interested — *because I guess she's a pervert.*

She moved her eyebrows up and down like Pepe LePew and slid herself closer. "So what happened? What was it about?"

Her fingers fell to my chest and her nails began to slide along my skin. I shivered, but not in a good way. Images of sloppy oatmeal and even sloppier old man flesh fired in connections of my brain. When I shivered, it wasn't because I was turned on.

My wife took notice. "I thought you had a sex dream? Are you okay?"

"I did."

"Then what's the...? Wait. You know what? I don't want to know."

My wife has lived with me a very long time and she understands all too well that some questions are better left unanswered.

-Steven Novak-

FIRST BOOK

FIRST BOOK

The first children's book I ever illustrated was titled *Sleeping Tiger*. The book is no longer in print, and I believe the publisher has long since folded.

Maybe it had something to do with my illustrations? Maybe? *Naw.*

I was overjoyed when I originally got the offer to work on the book. I was still working as a graphic designer at the local paper, and the book was not only going to be a fantastic change of pace, but maybe a big break for me as well. Sure, the publisher was tiny, and sure, they were local, and they weren't offering me much money or a decent amount of time to produce the work.

I didn't want to spend the rest of my life doing ads for local video stores that still offered Beta movies in their selection, though. *I had to take a shot.*

Plus, it was a job drawing, not designing with a mouse in my hand and Photoshop opened on my Mac. I'd need to break out my pencils. I'd need to dust off my paints. I was going to be lurched over my drawing table, diving in and letting it all hang out! I was going put everything I had into the book!

I was going to wow them! My work was going to be so damn amazing that it was going to take their whole company to the next level! Days after it hit the shelves I was going to have editors lining up outside my door! Anyone that needed illustrations for anything was going to be begging me to whip something up! Publishers across the country would be throwing bags of money with dollar signs through my bedroom window! I was going to be the next Chris-fucking-VanAllsburg! Nothing could stop me!

Well, as you might have already figured out, none of that happened. *None of what I ever think is going to happen, actually happens.*

Things started to fall apart when I received the story from my editor. The problem was that it sort of sucked. Actually, it didn't sort of suck as much as it really sucked. It sucked hard and fast, and it sucked looking for a quick and furious completion.

Despite this hurdle, I convinced myself that the story wasn't my problem. I had nothing to do with that, and in the end it wouldn't make an ounce of difference. Suck or not, I was going wow them with my illustrations. I was going to knock the illustrations so far out of the park that no one would be paying attention to the story anyway!

I began to work on my preliminary sketches that very night. My editor wanted to see them in a week, so I had to bust some ass. And bust ass I did. I didn't leave my drawing desk. When I got home from my day job I settled into the office chair and worked into the wee hours of the morning. Sleep didn't matter and basic nutrition was no longer necessary. Nothing was going to stop me. Nothing!

Though the sketches were *technically* due at the end of the week, I turned those *sumsvabitches* around in four measly days. Four days!

I'd drawn and redrawn, and worked and tweaked, and tightened and retightened until I settled on what I believed to be the absolute best way to convey the story and polish the turd. It was an impressive feat and the work was some of my best. *I was proud of myself, damn it.*

The next day I called my editor and told him I was faxing over the sketches.

"You're done already? Wow, great! Send them over and we'll take a look and get back to you tomorrow sometime."

Before leaving for work the next morning I sent everything over and prepared myself for the rush of accolades that would undoubtedly follow.

Tomorrow came and there was no call. *What the hell?*

He should have been doing backflips in his office, shouldn't he? When he laid his eyes on those sketches he should have knocked over furniture and taken his buddies out for a beer to celebrate his incredible stroke of luck. He should have been so happy that he'd stumbled across this diamond in the rough of an artist in the middle of nowhere, and yet he hadn't even picked up the phone.

Maybe he was hung over from all the partying and took the day off?

The following day the much-anticipated call finally arrived. Mr. Editor didn't sound quite as happy as I expected him to.

"Yeah, um. I've gotta tell you, Steven, this...well. Um, this is just not at all what we were expecting. In fact, I really can't think of anything nice to say about this. Listen, I'm thinking that maybe we'll give you a chance to fix these up, but I don't know. If we don't see significant improvements in the next batch, I think things might not work out."

"So no backflips then?"

Okay, so I didn't respond with the backflip thing. I was thinking it, though.

I was thinking that and *Holy shit, I'd love to smash this guy's face so hard that when I pull my hand back I am wearing his brain as a boxing glove.*

They faxed over a laundry list of stupid changes and I reworked the sketches while cringing and taking into consideration each and every one. The revised sketches looked awful. I faxed them his way a few days later.

(The fact that I keep typing the word "fax" is really dating me, isn't it?)

A day later I received another call. "These are much better, Steven. We love them."

Ain't that grand, because I fucking hated them.

To this day I still can't look at the finished book because I dislike the illustrations so much. It's easily the worst work I've ever done, and it's got my name right there on the cover.

*Annoyedgrumble

So what exactly is the moral of the story?

Simple: Don't bother doing your best work, cause no one gives a shit.

Okay, maybe that's actually not the moral. I just thought it sounded funny.

THOSE DAMN PUPPETS GET ME EVERY TIME

THOSE DAMN PUPPETS GET ME EVERY TIME

I don't really cry that much. In fact, I'm not really what you would call an "emotional person." My lack of emotion is a little frightening, really.

Let me just make it clear that I'm not against people who display their emotions without a care in the world. In fact, I think it's sort of impressive, in the way someone still sporting a Members Only jacket in 2001 was impressive.

I was raised in a household where crying just wasn't allowed. Wieners and wimps and "queer boys" cried. Big boys didn't cry. Big boys never cried. If big boys cried, big boys got the belt.

Through a sore red ass and a face full of tears, I learned long ago that's it was much easier for all involved if I bottled my emotions, glued the lid of the bottle shut, and stuffed the bottle down my throat with a lusty smile like a porn star taking a thirteen inch hog. *That's what big boys did.*

I am fully aware that this emotional deep-throating could one day come back to bite me in the ass. All the nonsense and resentment that I've stuffed deep inside my belly will undoubtedly rise to the top some day and explode from me in a torrent of rage and hate more nasty and vile than a Donald Trump rant about Rosie O'Donnell.

The chances of me waking up one morning, strewn across the bloody torsos of my loved ones and their heads arranged on my floor in the next room in a grotesque pentagram shape are fairly good. *I'll do my best to make sure it never comes to that, but some things are inevitable.*

As emotionless as I might sometimes be, I'll admit that there are a few things in the world that can successfully crack my normally stone-faced exterior.

Want an example? No? *Too bad. You're getting one, smartass.*

A while back, my wife and I were sitting in bed flipping though the channels, quickly coming to the realization that we have very little in common when it comes to our television preferences.

The Real Housewives of Theyshouldallbeshotintheface? Really, hun?

Anyway, after weeding through seven hundred channels of crap, I actually spotted something that interested me and told my wife to stop clicking. "Wait a minute. Stop there. Let's watch that."

"The Simpsons? Steven, I don't want to watch this. You've seen this episode a hundred times, anyway."

"So what? Mr. Burns wears loafers that are former gofers and sings a jaunty little ditty about it. It's hilarious."

"No."

"Fine. Whatever."

"Oh, let's watch this!"

"No I don't think so. We don't watch Nancy Grace in this house."

"What's wrong with Nancy Grace?"

"Let's see...one, she's annoying. Two, she has nothing important to say, but thinks that everything that comes out of her mouth is exactly that. Three, her sad attempt to keep her head in an annoying three-quarter profile is annoyingly awkward. And four, she's obsessed with dead babies. If I don't get the Simpsons, you don't get this idiot."

After surfing around a bit more and going through the channels we'd already gone through, my wife decided to peruse the movie options. As luck would have it, Showtime was showing *The Muppets Take Manhattan*.

My eyes latched onto Kermit's skinny green legs and Gonzo's oddly erotic blue penis nose and I was immediately compelled to watch. "Wait, leave this on."

I love the Muppets. I always have and I always will. The Muppets are pure and honest and if you dislike the Muppets you have way more problems than me. Also, just so we're clear on this point, despite liking the Muppets I do in fact have a penis. It exists. I was born with it. *It's not freaky, or weird, or creepy looking either*. It wasn't surgically attached to me after I graduated college and after I had my womanly parts sewn up. It's a 100% real, flesh and blood penis. Sometimes there's a lot more blood than flesh down there. *Especially when a Salma Hayek movie is involved*.

Being well aware of my intense, sometimes creepy Muppet-love, my wife decided to keep her opinions to herself and let me watch. She handed over the remote and strolled to the computer across the room with a defeated sigh.

It was still early on in the movie, and the gang was having some problems finding a producer for their Broadway show, *Manhattan Melodies*. Out of options, they eventually came to the heart-wrenching decision that maybe it was time they went their separate ways. This of course led into the singing the song *Saying Goodbye*. They hugged. They waved sadly and whispered teary puppet goodbyes. Within seconds my eyes were watering. I try to stop it from happening, I really did.

Unfortunately, much the same as pre-mature ejaculation, once the tears had started to squirt, holding them back became next to impossible. It was going to happen. Nothing could stop it. Thinking about baseball wasn't going to work. Picturing myself in a creamy, sweaty, stanky-crotch fivesome with the ladies of The View wouldn't have accomplished a thing. Even the addition of Dr. Phil to the View orgy would have no effect.

I was done for.

My wife spotted my pansy girl tears from across the room with her damn beady eyes. "Steven? Steven, are you crying?"

I bit my tongue and turned my head away. "No. What are you talking about?" I wasn't going to give her the pleasure. "Don't be stupid. I'm not crying, why would I cry? It's not like there's anything to cry about going on."

Sniffle.

Shit! I sniffled!

I thought about my father. I thought about his *spankin' belt* and tried to imagine I was Chuck Norris. Chuck Norris wouldn't be crying. The universe cries for Chuck Norris, not the other way around. I thought that if I could stop the tears before they got out of hand my wife would never notice; I could chalk it up to allergies or something. I needed to focus. I needed to steady myself and grow a pair! I needed to knuckle the hell up!

Unwilling to simply let it go, and anxious to toss a bit of mockery my way, the wife rose from her chair and began moving in my direction. I immediately dug my face into the blanket and smeared away my shameful wet while cursing Jim Henson and his damn cute plush pals though sniveling lips.

The wife reached my side of the bed and tried to pull the blanket from my quivering maw. "You are! Oh my God! You're crying at the Muppets! You're really crying at the Muppets!"

My nose was running. My eyes were burning and my hands were shaking. My eye make-up was running as we—

Err, no. Did I just type the word make-up? That was a mistake. My fingers were greasy with the remnants of a manly rib dinner. *Forget you saw that.*

The very next day I went to Jim Henson's grave, dug up his body and urinated on his dusty old bones.

Okay, so I never actually did that. *It would have been funny if I had, though.*

I hate the Muppets.

No I don't.

Yes I do.

No. No, I can't.

I'm sorry I said that.

COOL GUY HAIR ON A DUMB ASS GUY

COOL GUY HAIR ON A DUMB ASS GUY

I'm not exactly what you would call a "vain" person. In fact, I sort of hate myself.

I'm a simple man. I always have been. I don't pay too much attention to my appearance, or keep up on things like grooming or basic personal hygiene, and I really don't care what people think about me. There was a time when I did, sure.

I'm in my thirties now, though. Who gives a crap? I'm happy the way I am these days and I don't really have an interest in improving, or growing, or becoming someone else.

"You know what, Steven? I think it's time we gave you a new look." That was my wife talking to me.

New look? What the hell was this broad babbling about?

"What?"

"A new look. I think we should do something different with your hair."

Was she high? Was there asbestos leaking at work, slowly frying her brain to a crispy crunch? *She had to be high.* Completely out of the blue she was tossing some "new look" garbage at me like a greasy, stinky bucket of Kim Kardashian menstrual chum. *She was definitely smoking something.*

As a rule, I generally don't give two farts about my hair. *One fart, maybe. Two farts, never.* I don't comb my hair in the morning. I don't use a blow dryer and I don't spritz it with hair spray. I generally just step out of the shower and let it fall where it falls.

I'm lazy. So what? I don't care. I'm not trying to impress anyone, because I'm already married; it's mostly a lost cause, and I think people are stupid, anyway.

Farmer John doesn't wake up at 6AM to comb the hair of his goats, does he? Nope. That would be silly. A goat is exactly what it is. It's a naturally ugly, can-eating, foul-smelling, steel-burping, mud-standing, grass-crapping, disease-ridden bag of goop and blood. The act of parting its hair to one side won't make a difference.

In college I shaved my head bald every couple of weeks. *Those were the good old days.*

The problem was that my little brother was getting married in a few weeks and I was going to be his best man. I didn't think he wanted me to be mistaken for the hobo that wandered into the ceremony, so I agreed to let my wife have her stylist friend, Sherri, take her scissors to my head. Not only that, but I agreed to give the woman free reign to do whatever the hell she wanted to with me.

That takes balls: big brass ones. Big, hairy brass ones.

What was the worst that could happen? Maybe Sherri could indeed polish turds.

The appointment was on a Saturday. My wife and I arrived on time and were firmly planted on our asses waiting for the hair debacle to begin. She was leafing though some magazines filled with pretty boys with pretty hair, each of them with their shirts off and their lips puckered and their chest moist with just a hint of spray bottle sweat. They were standard male model stuff created to get the girls who like boys wet, and the boys who like boys — um, drippy? *I guess?*

She started tossing all sorts of questions my way while pointing at various pictures and absent-mindedly letting her fingers drag across the perky man nipples. "Do you like this one?"

"No, but I'm sure you do."

"Shut up. How about this one?"

"Not really, no."

"Ooh! This one would look good! What do you think?"

I shook my head. "Please don't make me look so goofy that I'm going to want to kick my own ass."

After a bit of back and forth we decided on something—and by "we" I of course mean "my wife and her pal."

Moments later it was go time.

Ten minutes into the process of making the goat look presentable, Sherri was painting strands of my hair and wrapping them in foil. I went from reluctantly forcing myself to get a haircut at the local *Fantastic Sam's* once every six months, to getting sections of it colored in a hipster salon downtown.

Maybe the place would burn down. *I started to pray for a fire.*

Fifteen minutes after that, I had a bowl on my head and some hot ass red lights were cooking my perfectly seasoned scalp like a baked potato.

No, no, no. This was a very bad idea. I should have never agreed to this. This was a bad idea and this wasn't going to end well.

For the briefest of moments I actually considered lifting the cooking pot from my head and running for the door. I pictured myself knocking people over and tearing the foils from my hair on the way out. I also considered punching Sherri in the face.

Another fifteen or twenty, or thirty or forty minutes elapsed, and I was at the rinsing sink with my head tilted backward uncomfortably and some guy shampooing my scalp. Not only was a dude massaging my scalp, but he had a remarkably tender touch. He had soft hands and firm fingers. The way he moved his fingers; it was hypnotic. It was…

Sweet lord, what the hell had I gotten myself into?

Five minutes later, the cutting began. Sherri trimmed and snipped, and pulled and snipped some more. She sprayed my hair and lifted it straight. She pulled what looked like a razorblade from her utility belt and primped the edges. In no time at all, the floor was covered with the remnants of my nonchalant past.

Twenty minutes after that, it was over.

My hair was suddenly spiky. In just a few hours it had transformed into some sort of faux-hawk, poseur, teenage hipster disaster. I'd transformed from a goat to Tyler Durden.

It was a *cool guy* haircut - no doubt about it. It was the sort of haircut that belonged in a magazine or dance club. *Shit.* Did I need to start going to raves? I didn't want to go to a rave.

A cool guy hair cut on a dumb ass guy. It was a recipe for disaster.

The wife liked it. My mother liked it. The people at my brother's wedding liked it, and I even got compliments on it on the rare occasions I ventured into the sun.

In the end I decided to keep the *cool guy* haircut. I didn't go to any raves though – or punch Sherri – or burn down her salon.

I think it made it easier for my wife to fantasize that I was one of those pert-nipple jokers in the magazines, though. So that has to count for something.

Goats Eat Cans Volume 2

TO THE VICTOR GO THE SPOILS

TO THE VICTOR GO THE SPOILS

"I feel sorry for you, Steven."

"Oh, yeah? Why's that?"

"Because of how badly you're about to lose."

"I'm not going to lose."

"Oh yes you are. You're going to lose, and you're going to feel pretty silly about it after it happens."

She'd been telling me that I was going to lose for nearly half an hour, ever since we plopped our rumps into the seat of the car. It got worse when we hit the highway. She was like a parrot. She wouldn't shut up.

"I'm not going to lose, hun."

She laughed so hard she nearly choked on her tongue. Her head fell back and her mouth opened wide. Her gestures were over the top and cartoonish. "You have no idea what you're getting yourself into, do you? I'm the mini-golf master, Steven. I mean it. You're going to feel really silly, really soon."

Miniature golf.

The wife and I had decided on a whim to head to a local Putt-Putt place and go head to head on the field of champions. When I suggested it, I did so because I thought it might be a fun way to kill some time on a particularly dull Saturday afternoon. My wife, however, took it as a declaration of war.

In the time since, she had made it clear in no uncertain terms that she wanted to crush me. She wanted to grab me by my nuts and twist until I screamed. She wanted to kick me in those very same nuts, grab hold of my Johnson, pull it between my legs and give me a dong wedgie. She wanted to emasculate me. She wanted to make me feel foolish, and she was going to enjoy doing it.

Apparently she had played a game twenty-years-ago (in the heyday of miniature golf) and beaten a couple of her friends. She was expecting to mop the green with me. She was already picturing planning out her victory dance. She might have even written up a speech.

I'd bitten my tongue long enough. "If you're so sure that you'll win, why don't we make it interesting?"

"Okay, you've got it. You want to make it interesting? Fine. I'd love to make it interesting. What do you have in mind?"

"Oral satisfaction."

"What?"

"If I win, I get oral satisfaction."

"You're a pervert."

"What does it matter, if you're so sure that you'll win?"

"It doesn't. Fine. Whatever. What do I get when I win?"

"What do you want? Oral satisfaction?"

"No. I would like a foot massage."

"Fine."

"A foot massage and a back rub."

"Fine."

"A foot massage and a back rub, and I want you to pumice stone my heels at least once a week for the next month."

"That's a little much."

"That's the deal."

"Fine."

When she shook my hand she grabbed it with both of hers and squeezed it hard. *Jerk.*

When I pulled into the parking lot, she drove her knuckles into my shoulder like a grade school bully. "Hope you're ready for this."

After we paid, she whacked me in the ass with her club. "Here it comes."

On the way to the first hole she tried to trip me. "Have a nice trip?"

I didn't actually trip, and I tried to explain to her that the joke didn't actually make sense unless I tripped. She didn't seem to care.

When we arrived at the hole, she stepped aside, smirked, and cocked her head in such a pompous sort of way that I suddenly wanted to stuff her into the miniature windmill on hole number eight. I didn't think she'd fit, but I would have had fun trying to make her.

"Ladies first." She winked when she said it.

On second thought, I wanted to feed her to the mechanical pirate head on hole number ten.

After I hit my ball, my wife chuckled, covered her mouth and turned her head.

Sure, it wasn't a great shot, but it wasn't a bad one either. It was a par three and my shot was certainly good enough to keep me on track for that.

She placed her ball and poked me in the chest with her finger. I think she might have bruised my ribs. "Is that all you got?"

She licked her finger and held it in the air to test the breeze. "Because if that's all you've got, you're in for a very long day, Steven ."

I imagined myself feeding whatever the pirate didn't want to eat to the balsa wood crocodiles in the pond situated in the center of the course. They looked hungry.

When my wife wrapped her fingers around her club, I prayed for a lightning strike. When she twisted her wrists and pulled back, I hoped her arms would break and flop in the breeze like one of those inflated men outside of a used car dealership. When she finally tapped the ball, I pictured a sinkhole opening up beneath her and swallowing her whole.

Turns out I didn't need any of that.

Her ball ricocheted off one of the little stone pillars blocking the way to the cup, popped up and landed in the grass ten feet away. Apparently she sucked at mini-golf.

It was a terrible shot. Scratch that, it was worse than terrible. It was atrocious. It was so bad that I almost thought she was joking.

She wasn't joking though. "Wait, wait! No! That's a do-over!"

As I watched my wife lean over some bushes to retrieve her ball, it was my turn to chuckle. I was already planning my victory dance. I was thinking about a speech. Being the good sport that I am, I even gave her a "do-over."

It didn't make any difference. Her do-over ended up at the bottom of the pond.

Her second do-over was much closer to the cup — *the cup on the second hole anyway.*

The oral satisfaction was a lock.

My wife spent the day eating her words and coming up with excuses. When we reached hole number five her knees were hurting and had been for the past week. Apparently it was throwing off her balance, which was in turn having an effect on her overall game. *Silly wife. She had no game.*

By the time we made it to seven her back was sore and the wind was in her eyes. *It wasn't windy.*

When she teed off on twelve the club was faulty, so she went to get a new one. *The new one didn't make any difference.*

By the time we made it to sixteen, the game of miniature golf was apparently a *"stupid game anyway."*

During the car ride home I pointed out on numerous occasions that she had more than doubled my strokes over the course of the game, and that didn't even count the various do-overs.

She called me a liar and claimed that I had fixed the scorecard because I was trying to be funny. When I reminded her that her wrist would be doing a hell of a lot more stroking later that night she called me a jerk.

Despite my mini-golf trouncing, I never actually did get my oral satisfaction. I also somehow ended up grinding away at her heels with a stupid pumice stone.

I should have fed her to the pirate.

THE AWKWARD BONER

THE AWKWARD BONER

When you're a kid, and you're a boy, pretty much anything can get your overexcited genitals to stand at attention. It doesn't matter what time of the day it is, or where you are, or who you're with. When it's going to happen, it's going to happen. The Rapture itself wouldn't stand a chance against it. One minute you're a ten-year-old kid on his way to school, when the sweet, oddly sensual vibrations of the seat beneath you causes your little guy to stand at attention. The bus swerves off the road, falls fifty feet and explodes, and suddenly you're standing at the gates of Heaven, trying desperately to disguise your excited shame with your shirt and praying that God won't notice.

"Steven? What's the problem down there, son? You know you can't bring that thing into Heaven with you, right? It's all cherubs and asexual angels up here, kiddo."

"I'm sorry. It was a bumpy road."

If God's a dude, He'd probably understand, but still, it would be pretty embarrassing.

Of course, in time a boy grows a little older and becomes a man, and gains at least some ability to control where and when the junior Cyclops decides to stretch his muscles.

At the time of this writing, I'm just entering my thirties. Everything is functioning as it should down below, for the most part. The gears are well-oiled, and there hasn't been too much of a need for a serious maintenance check. My submarine can dive, and it can surface, and it can still torpedo the hell out of the enemy. The only difference between Steven in his early thirties and that bus riding kid with the boner is that my penis and I are working together these days.

Well, most of the time, anyway. We're like a buddy cop movie. We started out hating each other, then we went through some pretty nasty shit, and now we're the best of pals.

Don't get me wrong; there are times when my pants partner is as confusing as the Architect's big speech at the end of The Matrix Reloaded. For example, lets hop in the Wayback Machine with Sherman and Mr. Peabody and comically spin our way a few years into the past.

I had just finished working out. I went into the bedroom and collapsed into a sweaty-sore heap of flesh on the bed. My arms and my legs and my lungs and every part of me was on fire. I couldn't breathe and I wanted to die. I didn't want to be touched, or spoken to, or talked about from another room. I needed to be left alone.

My wife wasn't on board with the plan. "Steven, give me some attention."

It sounded like something a four-year-old would say. It wasn't a four-year-old though, it was my wife. She was bored. She had been in the bedroom alone while I've been in the other room doing my workout thing, and she needed a distraction.

Damn it, I love my wife. I really do. I love her more than anything in the world and I would do anything for her. I was pretty fucking tired, though. "Give me like ten minutes to rest."

She folded her arms and scowled at me with raised eyebrows. "Nope. Attention now."

Before I could respond, she had hopped onto the bed beside me. The bouncing aggravated the cramp in my abdomen and I grimaced. Her hands went to my sweaty chest and her lips kissed my equally disgusting neck.

I smelled like a pile of dog plop fresh from a canine booty and plopped directly on top of an older pile of dog plop. I wasn't feeling sexy. I felt terrible. I groaned and tried to push her away.

She was not deterred. Instead she stepped up her rubbing efforts and doubled her grope ratio. Despite her attempts, nothing was happening. Nothing was stirring below. My little guy was as tired as me, and he wasn't buying what she was selling. There wasn't a *boing*, there wasn't a *poing*, and there definitely wasn't a *schwing*.

I felt like I'd just been run over by a truck. Of course nothing was happening down there. Nothing was going to happen down there, and even if something did start to happen, I was in no shape to do anything about it.

When her efforts to get me interested in anything other than silence and rest proved vain, a switch clicked in my wife's brain. Suddenly she turned from feeling amorous to feeling annoyed. The switch was quick; it was quicker than a drunken hummingbird popping out a booze-laden hiccup after a night on the town with some old college pals.

Her playful tickles transformed to slaps, and the slaps changed into closed-fist punches soon thereafter. She wasn't taking the rejection well. She grit her teeth and walloped me in the chest. She bit her lip and clubbed me on the arms. She snagged my wrist and delivered a particularly wicked Indian burn.

"Ouch! What the hell?"

"Oh, shut up, you baby."

She cracked me in the neck and backhanded me across the face. Realizing that I was too tired to fight back, the pace of her attack quickened. I became the recipient of an exceptionally stiff Charlie horse, and that was followed with an elbow to the kidneys. She grabbed the tip of my nose between two fingers and twisted. She stuck a pillow over my face and pressed down so hard that I couldn't breathe. She was like a crazy person. It was the whole "woman scorned" thing, and I was on the receiving end.

When she finally stopped it was because she was tired, tired of beating the piss out of me. She needed to take a break. I was throbbing all over. I had bumps on top of bumps, and there were even more bumps on top of those. I think I might have been bleeding internally. There was no sure way to tell.

"What the hell, Steven?"

"What? What's wrong now?"

"Where did this come from?"

I glanced down at my crotch. I was fully erect.

Hm. I guess I didn't notice that particular throbbing amongst the sea of throbbing that had become my body. There I was though, standing proud, and anxious, and ready to go.

It made no sense. Moments before I was getting the holy hell beat out of me in the least sexual manner a person could possibly imagine. It was a pain penis. I had a pain penis. There it was. The proof was in the pudding. A tribe of Indians had pitched a Tee-Pee in my pants and they were cooking a fine thanksgiving feast for the Pilgrims inside. *I'd become a pain penis guy.*

"Why do you have a boner, Steven?"

I didn't have an answer. "I dunno."

"When exactly did it happen? Was it when I was punching your shoulder? Or maybe it was when I slapped you in the face?"

I still didn't have an answer. "I'm not sure."

It was the truth. I wasn't sure and I didn't know. Was it possible that getting the beejezus beat out of me actually turned me on? I couldn't recall sporting wood when I was getting my ass kicked in high school. Did this mean I was going to have to start buying leather? And whips? What about one of those gimp suits?

Oh, shit. I really didn't want to wear one of those gimp suits.

The very next night my wife and I decided to go out for dinner. We were sitting outside the restaurant waiting for our names to be called when she turned to me and asked, "Are you sure you're okay to go in Steven?"

"What? Why wouldn't I be?"

"I don't know, you aren't going to get any boners while we're in there, are you?"

The following day I had to make a trip to the supermarket to pick up a few things.

"Be careful while you're there, Steven."

"What? Why?"

"I just don't want you getting any boners."

The next day she turned off the television while I was watching it.

"Hey! Turn that back on!"

"I was worried it might give you a boner."

When I was putting gas in the car she warned me about boners. When I was making dinner she asked me if the lettuce turned me on. A few weeks later I told her that I was going to write a story about my newly discovered pain penis.

"Be careful how you write it, Steven."

"Why?"

"I don't want you to get any boners."

She was never going to let me live it down.

(Pun intended.)

-Steven Novak-

PEOPLE WATCHING

PEOPLE WATCHING

A good deal of my time is spent watching people.

Don't worry, it's nothing creepy. My people watching doesn't usually involve a pair of high-powered binoculars and an apartment rented under a false identity that also happens to be located across the street from a Ladies Workout World.

I don't have a thing for MILFs with a little junk in the trunk.

Okay, so maybe I do. *That's neither here nor there, though.*

Anyway, as I was saying, I watch a lot of people. Why do I do it? I'm not sure, really. My guess is that is has something to do with the fact that I'm sort of anti-social, and because of that I'm never actually involved in conversations of my own—*you know, besides the ones in my head.*

That's where my real friends are. There's little Tito, and big Jermaine, and then there's Joey, and of course medium Joey and his identical twin, medium Joey II. There's even a tiny Eskimo lad I like to refer to as tiny Esk. Tiny Esk is always lugging around his freshly caught trout and he's always bundled up in his little furry jacket, and when he smiles at me he flashes that space between his two front teeth that I find so damn cute.

Sigh. *I love you most of all, little Esk.*

Enough about my make-believe friends. Let's get back to the story at hand.

On a Tuesday night a few years ago, my wife had a fever that was peaking at about 103, and I figured it was about time to lug her across town to urgent care. *You know, so she wouldn't die. At least not until all the life insurance forms had been properly filled out.*

The waiting room was filled to the brim. People were coughing, and hacking, and hunched over with bloody rags pressed to various parts of their bodies. It was standing room only, like a Kriss Kross concert in the early 1990s, or a weekend performance at the local state fair by that terrible band Billy Bob Thornton was a part of.

Okay, maybe those weren't the best examples.

After filling out the proper forms, I managed to snag a couple seats near the rear of the room the moment they became available. The woman sitting directly to my left was engaged in a conversation with the man sitting directly to her left. She couldn't have been a day over forty, and yet her skin looked like a dried out catcher's mitt. She smelled like potato salad — potato salad baked in a puddle of urine.

"So anyhows, I quit the smoking about eight-days- ago and suddenly I ain't got no more feelings in my fingers. I mean, I can move them, but I can't feel myself moving them. That make any sense to you?"

The guy on her left just nodded in agreement. *That's right, I typed "nodded in agreement."*

On the opposite end of the room there was a woman with two kids hanging from her like sickness-soaked sacks of laundry. The little girl lying against her chest looked terrible. There was a constant flow of snot leaking from her nose and oozing annoyingly slow shimmery boogerfall. I watched it the entire way.

I couldn't turn my head.

Her son slid himself from her grasp and began running in circles, screaming at the top of his lungs, and generally being a nuisance. "Tyler! Sit down! Sit down right this instant!" When she reached for him, he dodged her hand like a pro boxer avoiding a punch. "Mommy can't deal with this right now! You better sit down right now or I'm calling your father! I'll do it! I've got the phone right here! Do you want me to call him? Is that what you want, Tyler?"

Tyler laughed in her face and spun around like a top so fast that he lost his balance and flopped onto his butt.

I was suddenly reminded of just why I chose a vasectomy. I glanced briefly in the direction of my crotch and told my boys that I love them, but it was the best choice for all involved. *They nodded in agreement.*

Someone new entered the waiting room, and the catcher's mitt with the boobs recognized her immediately. "Hey girl! Hey! It's me!"

"Oh! Hey, girl! How are you?"

"Well, I ain't doing too good, I'll tell you what. You see, I quit smoking about eight- days- ago and suddenly I ain't got no feeling in my fingers." Somehow she managed to twiddle her ancient mummy fingers. "It's just gone. Can't feel anything. I think I might have had a stroke or something. No way of knowin' for sure, though."

I was really starting to hate this story.

Back on the other side of the room, Tyler's mom had managed to stop him from scooting around on the ground while making fire engine sounds. She asked him to come close. She claimed she had a secret to tell him.

"Tyler, see that door right there? You know who's behind that door? A man who spanks little boys."

Tyler wasn't buying it. "No there's not."

"Yes there is, and if you don't stop yelling, Mommy is going to tell him to come out here and spank you."

"You're a liar. There's no one back there."

"Oh, yes there is. Don't test me, Tyler. I'll tell him to come out here and spank you. I really will. Don't push me."

Tyler strolled defiantly over to the door his mother was pointing at and opened it up. Of course there was no one back there. He looked back at her, grinned, and stuck his tongue out.

The little bastard reminded me a bit of myself. Don't get me wrong, I still wanted to grab him by his neck and spin him like an airplane until his neck snapped.

He had moxie though. *I had to at least acknowledge the moxie.*

Defeated, his mother rolled her eyes and took the absolute deepest breath I think I've ever seen a human being take. In that moment, I could tell that she regretted getting drunk at her girlfriend's New Year's Eve party four-years-ago and thinking the rhythm method was legitimate.

My attention was drawn away from the terrible Tyler and his defeated shell of a mother when smoking woman unexpectedly turned in my direction. "Hey there."

Shit.

Shit. Poop. Diarrhea.

I didn't want to talk to this zombie-skinned broad, and I really didn't want to hear about the crazy "can't feel but can move her hand" situation that was brought on by a nonexistent stroke and had been caused by her quitting smoking eight-days-ago.

Crap. Double crap. Triple crap. How was I going to get out of this?

"Hi."

She extended her jittery, smoke-browned finger and pointed to my wife. "That your lady?"

"Yep." I responded, trying to keep my answers as short as possible. "That's my lady."

I looked away. I didn't want to make eye contact. I thought that if I didn't look at her she might get the idea and leave me alone.

"She doesn't look so good."

Nope.

I needed to end this and I needed to end it quickly. I could feel the thickness of her breath on my face. It was sticking to me like tar. It was soaking into my skin and melding itself to my pores. In thirty minutes I'd look exactly like her.

I did what I needed to do. "Yeah, she's running a really high fever. Plus, there's this strange thing happening with her hand. She can move it, but she can't really feel anything when she's moving it."

I'm sorry. I couldn't help it.

I can be a real smart ass sometimes. I can also be a jerk. I had to do it. I had to make it clear in no uncertain terms that I wasn't interested in hearing abou—

"Really? Ohmygawd! I have the exact same thing! You see, I quit smoking eight-days-ago because I decided I wanted to be around to see my daughter grow up..."

Was this woman for real?

Suddenly the screaming little freight train that I'd come to know as Tyler slammed into my legs while trying to do a handstand and babbling something about Pikachu. Or maybe it was Timmy O' Toole? Or little boys' ear gruel? Now that I think of it, it might have been "skaters rule."

Needless to say, the next time my wife gets sick she's staying at home. If that means she has to die then I guess she'll just have to die.

I should have all the insurance forms filled out by then, anyway.

I SOMETIMES LET MY WIFE DRIVE

I SOMETIMES LET MY WIFE DRIVE

Generally, when the wife and I take to the highway, which is a pretty rare occurrence, I'm the one behind the wheel. This isn't because I have a penis and I think that it takes a penis to operate a motor vehicle. *Driving a car with a penis would be difficult, even for those most gifted in the dong area.*

The truth is that, despite my penis, I don't like cars and I hate driving. It's boring, and it's cramped, and dealing with the idiots on the road is a pain in the ass. Plus, there's nowhere I want to go. If I don't want to go anywhere and I don't like the act of getting there, what's the point? *There isn't one.*

I've also never changed a tire or oil, or even opened a glove compartment.

Actually, I have done the last thing once or twice.

There are two reasons I insist on driving when the only other person in the car is my wife. Want me to list them? No? Well, I'm going to do it anyway. If you didn't want to read my ramblings you probably shouldn't have bought this book, and you definitely shouldn't have made it this far into it.

The first is that my wife gets nervous every time a truck passes her on the highway, and every time she gets nervous, she nearly drives us off the road. Seriously, in eleven years of marriage we're averaging two close call collisions into the midway per season. *It's amazing there aren't multiple shards of windshield embedded in my brain yet.*

The second reason I don't like to let my wife behind the wheel is because she seems to think she knows exactly where she's going, when in truth, she knows very little. The problem is that she's lived in southern California her entire life. She thinks she knows every secret back road, shortcut, and quicker route home that there is to know. She thinks she's smarter than the GPS and the various satellites feeding the GPS its information. That's right, she thinks she's smarter than the billion dollar computers floating in space.

This is a woman who isn't yet sure how to empty the trash can on her laptop.

On this particular occasion, when my wife opened her hand, motioned for the keys, and said to me, "I know a shortcut. It'll get us home in half the time," she seemed oblivious to just how silly she sounded.

I knew she was going to get us lost and she knew that I knew that she was going to get us lost. The car even knew she was going to get us lost and the keys clung to my palm like sticky candy to the grubby-fat palm of a pudgy baby.

Needless to say, I was reluctant. I tried to shoo her away. "No, it's okay. It's not like we're in a hurry or anything. I've got it."

"Stop it, Steven. Come on. Give me the keys."

I should have shoved her over. *That's exactly what I should have done.* I should have walloped her in the chest with both hands and slammed her to the pavement. When her skull hit the cement, it might have knocked her unconscious. Once she'd been neutralized, I could have rolled her into the trunk, drove us home, and saved us both the misery of what was to come.

Unfortunately, I did the exact opposite.

Her eyes narrowed and she motioned for the keys once again. "Come on, Steven. Give me the keys." She meant business.

With a sigh and a shake of my head, I handed over the keys. *I really need to start walloping people more.*

We were on the highway for less than five minutes when she pulled off.

"Where are you going, hun?"

"It's a shortcut. Trust me."

Before continuing, I should mention that we were only half an hour away from our destination to begin with. We didn't have a long trip ahead of us. We weren't traversing the country by covered wagon and stopping at night to cook beans from a can and blast a buffalo in the face for protein. There wasn't a chance that either of us was going to die of dysentery along the way. The car was air-conditioned. It was comfortable. There was a bag of fun-sized snickers in the back seat.

In a roundabout sort of way, the *regular* cut was actually a *shortcut*.

The wife wasn't hearing it, though. She thought she knew a quicker way home and damn it she was going to take it!

Ten minutes into the journey it was fairly clear to the both of us that we were lost. The direct route the highway provided was a distant memory. Even if we had wanted to turn around and go back the way we came, we wouldn't have been able too. We'd been wandering for too long and we'd past the point of no return.

I felt like I needed to say something. "We're lost, aren't we?"

"No. Stop it. I know exactly where we're going."

I wasn't buying it. A blind man with one deaf ear, the inability to speak, a pack of rodents living in his lower intestine, and wooden pegs where his arms should be wouldn't have bought it. *My wife is a terrible actress.*

She was nervous. She wiped a bead of sweat from her face, tried her damndest to erase the look of utter confusion from her face, and turned on the radio. Some terrible 80s song began to play and she threw one hand into the air like she'd just stepped into the hottest club in town and she owned the place. "Alright! I love this song!"

I still wasn't buying it. It was a distraction. She was trying to throw me off the scent and it wasn't going to work. No one likes old Bananarama songs that much. *Not even Bananarama.*

Fifteen minutes later, the sun began to set. The car jumped and the road turned to gravel. Our tires were spitting dirt, and there were rocks banging against all of the *car-stuff* on the underside.

I think I heard a piston pop. *I dunno what it was.* Something popped.

Before I could say a word, my wife held up her hand and pointed her palm at my face. "Not a word, Steven! Don't you dare say a word! The turn is right up here. Three more blocks and we're there!"

My only problem was that there didn't seem to be anything even vaguely resembling "blocks" where we were.

We passed by a fence that looked like it had been constructed in the early 20s from the bones of dead cowboys. I swear I saw a femur. There was a dead raccoon twisted in the barbed wire, binding them all together and blowing in the breeze like a pirate flag. *It was a warning.*

Five minutes later I spotted a rusted Port-A-Potty in the middle of an empty field. Rip Van Winkle himself peeked out from the door and flashed us the finger. *I think I might have seen his junk.*

When the sun dropped from the sky I began to get worried. We'd been four-wheeling through the backwoods of DeliveranceTown for nearly an hour. Sure, we hadn't yet been kidnapped and butt raped by the locals, but it was bound to happen sooner or later. I've heard that hillbilly butt rape happens most often at night. Trust me on this. *I read it in a pamphlet.*

From the darkness outside, something howled. I can't say for certain if it was a wild dog, or a wolf, or some poor, unsuspecting sap bent over the backdoor of a pickup truck getting his fudge packed more awkwardly than Lucy and Ethel at the chocolate factory. It was one of those things, though.

Something smacked against the window and we both jumped, and my wife laid into the gas. Suddenly the car was swerving, careening back and forth and tearing into the uneven ground beneath us. A flash of lightning exploded over the mountains. Something laughed. The radio went dead and something that sounded like a lion roared. I think I even heard a gunshot.

I was seconds from leaning over, walloping my wife in the face, taking the wheel, and getting us the hell out of whatever circle of hell we'd accidently driven into when the gravel road transformed, quite suddenly, again into pavement. A streetlight popped into existence just over the horizon and three more followed soon after. A couple minutes later my wife maneuvered the car back into civilization.

Not only were we on a street I recognized, but we were also ten minutes from home. A trip that should have lasted thirty minutes at the most, had taken us nearly an hour and a half.

My wife turned to me and smiled brightly. "See? Told you I knew where I was going."

I think she actually expected me to buy it. *The woman's got balls.*

PISSED OFF AND PISSING BLOOD

PISSED OFF AND PISSING BLOOD

It was sometime in the early afternoon that I began feeling an altogether uncommon ache in my man marbles.

When I say *ache* in this instance, I'm not referring to that good sort of *ache* I sometimes get when watching pretty much anything with Rosario Dawson in it. No, this was something entirely different. This was something ugly. This was something even Rosario's leathery-small outfit in Sin City couldn't fit.

By the time four o'clock rolled around my dangly warbles began getting warm. The warming sensation quickly morphed into something more closely resembling the word *hot,* and once again this wasn't any sort of hot I was accustomed to or enjoying. It was certainly nothing like the hot explosion of orgasmic bliss one might experience after a week-long viewing of various Rosario Dawson flicks set to repeat on an endless, sexy loop.

No, this was an ugly *hot*. This was a weird *hot*. This was an unnatural, worrisome, on the verge of burning *hot*.

It was like a chimpanzee dressed in 70s booty shorts and wearing a pair of roller skates, who also happens to have an impressively firm pair of DDs, and is going down on the corpse of Dom DeLuise.

This *hot* was just plain wrong.

Despite the overwhelming feeling of dread, I told myself to ignore it and go on with my day. I needed to stop being a wimp and I needed to knuckle up. It would all go away eventually. It had to. Nothing was wrong. It had to go away and it would. I just needed to ignore it.

It worked for Nancy at the end of the first "Nightmare on Elm Street," right?

Let's cut to a bit later in the day.

The sun had long since gone down, and I was sitting on the bed taking in a rather comical rerun of The Simpsons. My loving wife was at her computer on the opposite end of the room sifting through the wonderfully *genius* mind of Perez Hilton. *Ha! Ha! Ha! He used MS Paint to draw something that sort of, kind of resembles cum on Paris Hilton's lips! Oh look, he did the same thing to John Mayer! It says "slut" over Lady Gaga's head! The man's a genius!*

Hopefully the sarcasm is hitting you harder than a juiced young Lou Ferrigno sporting a pair of brass knuckles and pimp slapping you across the face.

Just as Homer was blasting zombie Shakespeare into a pile of 2D bones, a wave of unbearable pain stabbed me in the lower back so hard that for a moment I thought I might have transformed into a "lady of the night" in 1880s London, and Jack The Ripper was attempting to hack me into pieces small enough to fill a Hot Pocket.

I rolled from the bed and hit the floor with a thump. Almost instantly I popped up and wobbled into the hallway. The pain in my lower back was shooting up my side and moving into my arm.

Suddenly I had Tourette's. "What the fuck? Motherfucker you've got to be kidding me! What the shit?" I was slamming into walls and punching myself in the side in a pathetic attempt to beat the pain out of me. *I succeed only in angering it further.*

"Okay, I'm sorry! I'm sorry I punched you! Please just stop, please stop!"

In an instant I transformed into one of those women who stand by their man even though he enjoys pounding her into the pool table as much as he does Sunday Night Football. I was pleading with the awful, bastard son of a bitch pain having its way with my insides. I was begging it and offering sexual favors. It chuckled at how much of a pussy I was and stabbed me harder to prove a point.

My wife miraculously managed to pull herself away from some terribly important information about what Kim Kardashian wore to VH1's "Reality TV Awards" and followed me into the hallway.

"Steven, what's wrong? Are you okay? What's wrong? Is it a cramp?"

Yes – it's a cramp. Of course, that makes perfect sense. I always react to cramps the same way JFK's head reacted to the bullet from Oswald's gun: by turning it into a sloppy bowl of clam chowder and human hair.

If this was a cramp, it was the Andre the Giant, the Godzilla, the Mothra, and Manute Bol of cramps. This wasn't simply a cramp. This was the end of days.

I dropped to my knees and bit down on my lower lip. I inhaled deeply and tried my damndest to get a handle on the flashes of pain moving into my legs like the German army into Poland. Above me the wife continued to blather. In all our years of marriage she'd never seen me like this, and I could tell she was finally starting to get worried.

I had little time to fret over her fragile emotional state, however. The pain was getting worse. It had moved into my back and was bouncing around like the gyrating hips of Satan himself during his Wednesday night bellydancing class at the adult annex.

In a heartbeat things went from *bad* to *really bad,* and finally to *sweet shit how can it get any worse!* Suddenly I was in the prison shower and I'd just dropped the soap.

Overcome with the feeling of a four-hundred-pound dude with a Che Guevara tattoo sliding his dry-as-a-bone *spontz* into my virgin hole, I looked up at my wife and muttered, "Get the car."

Twenty minutes later I was pacing back and forth in the emergency room mumbling to Jesus, Buddha, Kirk Cameron, or anyone else willing to listen and make the pain stop. I told myself that I'd believe in all the nonsense they wanted me to if they would just make the pain go away.

Thirty minutes later I was urinating into a cup and noticing that my urine didn't look very much like urine at all. *It looked a whole hell of a lot like blood, though.* It was thick, and it was shiny, and it was as red as a woman's discharge during a "heavy flow." The disgusting liquid was squirting from me like acid-stink cherry pudding.

The only problem was that my life wasn't a horror film, and I wasn't a classic 1980's Tom Savini effect.

Unless my sixth grace health teacher had been feeling lazy and skipped a chapter, I was fairly positive blood wasn't supposed to come from there.

An hour or so later I was told that I had a pair of stones in one of my kidneys. Rambunctious little rapscallions that they were, it seemed they'd decided to throw a little party and make a mess of the place. I shook my head and told myself that as soon as I saw them, they were *so grounded.*

As luck would have it, I had an opportunity to see them face to face a week or so later, moments after the pointy-edged scamps tore their way through my urethra and shot through the too-small eye of my penis in one of those wonderful, blinding moments of pain we rarely get to experience in life.

I think one of them might have etched his name in the wall on the way out.

The other one just wrote "LOL! KEWL! PeReZ RuLZ!"

Everyone is reading that schmuck.

-Steven Novak-

SLEEP FIGHTING

SLEEP FIGHTING

One minute I was fighting a clan of ninjas on the dark side of a planet in the furthest reaches of space, and the next I was lying in bed with my wife slapping me in the chest and screaming "Steven! Wake up! Wake up!"

Honestly, the space-ninjas were less terrifying.

Here's the deal. You see, I have an affliction, and that affliction is called sleep fighting.

I think sleep fighting is a real thing. I'm not sure though. I know I heard some guy mention it once on some show on that thing in my bedroom that broadcasts various forms of entertainment to the masses.

Believe it or not, I'm actually a pretty docile guy: maybe too docile, even.

I'm one of those "la-dee-da, nothing affects me," never raises his voice people who will one day explode and take to the streets with a belt full of grenades, an AK-47, and an overwhelming desire to see what your insides look like sprayed across the pavement. It's bound to happen. The same as night turns to day, day turns to night, and the world will come to an end in 2012, it's a done deal.

I like to keep things bottled up, and those bottled up emotions sometimes come out in unexpected ways.

My wife has been dealing with my sleep fighting for years. She's interrupted my dreams on numerous occasions to tell me that I was punching the air, or pounding my feet against the bed, or knocking things off the dresser. She even once told me that I picked up the cat and tossed it across the room.

I didn't feel all that bad about that one. *Our cats are assholes.*

While I can't imagine that my wife is okay with the fact that I like to duke it out with Apollo Creed and whip our pets around the room when I'm sleeping, I do think she's become accustomed to it.

It's part of her life now. She said "I do," She slipped the ring on her finger, and she used that very same finger to reluctantly massage my perineum.

Years ago she fell into the habit of sleeping with her head on the opposite side of the bed. *At least, until I whacked her in the face with my shin.*

She woke me up by slugging me in the stomach and ran into the bathroom holding her nose. "Damn it, Steven! Damn it! You kicked me in the dose!"

I didn't mean to laugh. I really didn't. She did say, "dose" instead of "nose" though. It's impossible not to chuckle at that. *Hell, I bet you chuckled when you read it.*

Fear not, those of you out there who love my wife and hate my guts. The little lady got her payback a few months later.

Because of the Ernesto Hoost-foot to the face incident, I was told to make sure that we were sleeping on the same side of the bed at all times, no matter how annoying or uncomfortable it might have been for me. I'm too tall to sleep with my head at the foot of the bed, and doing so folds my body like a crumpled corpse in the trunk of my car. Not that I have a corpse in my trunk or anything. No. That was just an example. It was. Seriously. Trust me. You don't need to go looking.

Since I didn't really *want* to bash my wife in the face, at least not most of the time, when push came to shove, I agreed.

That very night I found myself alone in the jungle. I was covered in mud and decked out in camouflage, and I was being hunted by a pack of Predators from the movie series of the same name. They'd been tacking me for hours and had me cornered. I was teetering on the edge of a ravine, the glow of their laser sights dancing on my rippling pecs when I charged the group of snarling uglies, launched myself into the air and delivered a flying kick to one of their faces. My attack connected and my foot exploded.

"Shit! God damn it!"

I felt like I'd been shot, like I'd stepped on a landmine and suddenly had the shrapnel of my big toe splattered on my face. The pain in my foot shot into my leg and continued its journey upward before boxing my testicles like a hungry young boxer working the speed bag.

I rolled off the bed and crashed to the floor. "Motherfucker! Mothershit! Damn it!"

The fact that I was cussing like a climaxing sailor after three years at sea immediately woke my wife. She clicked on the light, slid from the bed and scurried in my direction.

I was already on my feet—well, on one foot anyway. My other foot was in my hand, blood spurting from between my fingers as I hopped around the room and continued to cuss through clenched teeth.

My wife placed her hands on my shoulders, trying desperately to get me to stop bouncing like an anxious Tigger ready for a Pooh-related adventure. "What happened? Are you okay?"

When she spotted my blood-soaked hands, she immediately backed away. "Oh my— Wha-what happened?"

I hobbled past her and into the bathroom, where I turned on the shower and lowered my bloody foot into the spray. In no time at all the basin of the tub was coated in red. There was a hole in my flesh the size of a dime. The skin was frayed and gouged. The edges of the newly formed hole were already turning purplish-blue.

My wife was at the doorway, nibbling nervously on her fingers and watching as blood continued to spurt from my punctured limb. "Are you okay? What happened?"

Though I wasn't awake for the actual act, I utilized my incredible Sherlock senses and put the pieces together fairly quick. When I was fighting those Predators I was actually fighting the dresser next to the bed. Apparently I'd gone and kicked the pointy edge. *Stupid wife.*

It had nothing to do with her and I had no reason for being upset with her, but I was. *Stupid wife.*

"It was a Predator tooth."

It took her a minute or so to respond. "What?"

"A Predator tooth. They have sharp teeth."

I wrapped my foot and spent the next week and a half hobbling around the house like an idiot. My wife eventually figured out that it didn't have anything to do with a Predator tooth and I think she actually enjoyed watching me wobble like a gaslight drunkard hopped up on goofballs and silly sauce. She even chuckled a few times.

Stupid wife.

THE ART "EXPERIENCE"

THE ART "EXPERIENCE"

I'm terrible when it comes to face-to-face social interaction. I really am. I'm awkward and weird, and I generally make people feel awkward and weird because of my awkward weirdness.

Did hearing me admit that make you feel awkward and weird about what you're reading? *It did, didn't it? The proof's in the pudding.*

My ability to bring a party to a halt isn't exactly a new development. I've been this way for a very long time, and the chances of me ever being anything else are slimmer than Calista Flockhart's thighs or the possibility that Katy Perry will ever write a song that doesn't make me want to chop her head off and store her boobs in my freezer.

Wait just one cotton pickin' minute. *Did I just make a Calista Flockhart reference?*

Wait one more cotton pickin' minute. *Did I just say I wanted to chop off her head and store her boobs in my freezer?*

Wait one last cotton pickin' minute! *Did I just type the words "cotton pickin'" three times?*

I bet you're feeling pretty damn awkward and weird now.

Anyone that knows anything about me knows how utterly useless I am when it comes to situations in which human beings gather to do the things human beings do. It's common knowledge. It's also the reason I was so taken aback when my wife said the following to me over dinner one night: "So…we're doing this silent auction thing at school, and I signed you up for an art experience with some of the kids."

I nearly choked on my fork of spaghetti. "What?"

"Oh, it's nothing, Steven. You'll meet the winners in the classroom and give them an art lesson. You can show them how to paint or something. It'll be fun. You'll love it."

I jabbed the fork into my brain.

Okay, I actually didn't do that. I wanted to though. *It'll be fun? I'll love it?*

Was this broad insane? Who the hell did she think she was married to? I don't even have fun and love doing the things I actually have fun and love doing. I'm practically a Vulcan. I'm incapable of such emotions.

"Are you nuts? I'm not doing that."

Instantly the expression on her face changed. It twisted into something ugly. It coiled and morphed into that angry wife-thing that wives everywhere do when they mean business. If you're a man and you're married, you know what I'm talking about. You've seen it before. It haunts your dreams and makes your genitals run for cover. For some reason the name, John Bobbit popped into my head. *This was going to suck.*

Two weeks later, I found myself in her classroom after school, waiting for the *winners* to show up and the art "experience" to begin.

Unlike John Bobbit, my penis remained firmly attached: loosely actually. Maybe dangly would be more appropriate? *Whatever.* What I'm basically trying to say is that it hadn't been chopped off and tossed into the woods by a crazy woman.

I'd made the right choice.

Less than ten minutes later the kids arrived. There were four of them: all girls, and all under the age of ten. My wife gathered the group around a table at the rear of the room and I proceeded to kill time by filling a few glasses of water for them to dip their paintbrushes in. After I filled them once, I poured them out and filled them again. A quick glance at the clock told me I'd only wasted three minutes. I emptied and filled the glasses again. That killed another sixty seconds.

Damn it.

Why was I so nervous? They were just kids: snot-nosed little kids and nothing more. I was twice their size and, in at least one case, three times! I couldn't allow these kids to get the better of me. It was time to stop being such a sackless weirdo and grow a pair! It was time to knuckle up and be a man!

My hands were sweaty and my face flushed. I could feel their tiny little kid eyes watching me from across the room, staring at me and wondering why I was constantly refilling the same four plastic cups. They were talking in their little kid voices to each other: whispering. One of them laughed and another joined in.

Were they laughing at me? I bet they were laughing at me. *Those little punks.*

That's it! I'd had enough! I'd show them! I'd *experience* the crap out of that art "experience!" It was time to step up and knock this thing out of the park! It was time to point to the bleachers like Babe Ruth and swing for the fences! It was time to channel my inner Kirk and take on the Gorn, despite being grossly overmatched! It was time to stop making nerdy Star Trek references that were in no way helping my cause!

With my fully-filled plastic cups, I strode across the room with my chest puffed and my chin pointed north. I reminded myself once again that I was a grown-ass man and that my fear was idiotic. I needed to take charge! I needed to take control of my stupid brain and let it know exactly who was controlling whom!

I needed to fail miserably, despite my bravado! *Wait. What? Forget that last part.*

Barely five minutes into the "experience," and I was already a blubbering mess. I was sweating more than John Candy in a latex John Candy suit. Every sentence was a contradiction. My words were bumping and sliding into each other like drunken assholes in a mosh pit, molding and melding like glue and spurting from my mouth in mostly nonsensical grunts. Suddenly my hands wouldn't work. For the first time in my life I couldn't even draw. Hell, I could barely hold my pencil.

Not only were these kids getting the better of me, they knew something was wrong. The puddle of perspiration on the desk below my head was a dead giveaway.

The little girl with the wide eyes and confused look on her face across from me wasn't helping matters any. Her face was slimy. She kept smacking her lips and scratching her head, and dropping flakes of dandruff into the still wet paint below. Every once in a while her tongue would peek out from between her lips, extend upward, and try its damndest to find its way into her nose. *She really needed to stop doing that.*

In between my jittery pencil strokes and awkward burp-speak, I could hear laughter coming from elsewhere in the room, from behind me. Though the muscles in my neck had stiffened to the point of being utterly useless long ago, I managed to spot my wife and one of her teacher friends standing in the doorway with wide smiles on their faces. They were watching me suffer and they seemed to really be getting a kick out of it.

Wait one final cotton pickin' minute. This was all a set-up, wasn't it?

The girl sitting beside me broke wind. *Being married is fantastic.*

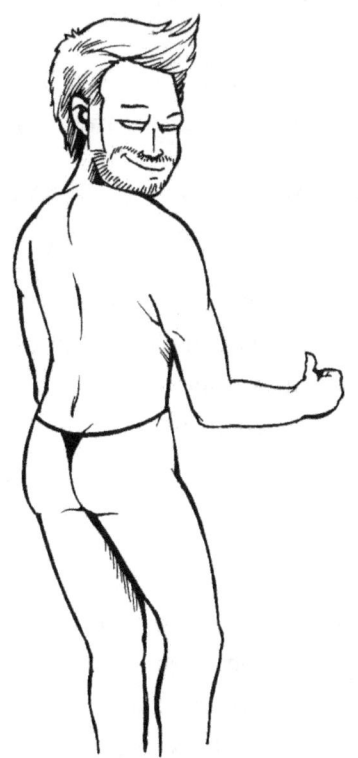

NOT THAT I'M BRAGGING OR ANYTHING

NOT THAT I'M BRAGGING OR ANYTHING

On Christmas morning a few years back, I discovered that my wife had stuffed a couple of *sexy* man thongs into my stocking.

It least I hope it was my wife—otherwise Santa Claus is a damn pervert.

One of them was shiny red with a zipper in the front, and it looked like it could have been somewhat dangerous if not treated with absolute care. The second was a leathery black material with a button-latch thingy on the front, and the third was tiger striped with tassels dangling from it.

Equally confused and aroused, I let one of them dangle from my finger and stared at it as my wife stared at me with a lecherous smile on her face from across the room. It was the sort of smile generally reserved for creepy guys who work rundown porn shops, construction workers who holler as the ladies walk by, or those select few who have the guts/stupidity to frequent rooms with glory holes.

Over the years the thongs have only been worn a couple times. Honestly, I just don't have the kind of confidence in my ass that's needed to fully pull off something like that on a weekly or even monthly basis. Without confidence, I'm just a chubby, bashful guy in a thong with a mildly dimpled butt, which isn't sexy to anyone, *anywhere*.

Fast forward to a couple years later. My wife had been away for a week and a half visiting family in another state, during which time I'd missed her immensely. I was anxious to see her again, and I wanted to surprise her when she stepped into the house, opened her arms, and came looking for a *welcome home* embrace.

I considered my options:

Surprise her with an elegant bouquet of flowers? *Naw. Too obvious.*

Present her with a well-chosen card and a box of chocolates? *Meh. Same problem as the flowers.*

Casino tokens and a dry martini? *Nope. She wasn't Frank Sinatra.*

A swift kick to the baby maker?

Hm. While that would have certainly surprised her, I'm not sure she would've appreciated it.

Then it hit me like a greased-up wiener at a butt-stank male strip club: *the thongs.*

I decided that I would greet her at the garage door the moment she arrived and I'd be wearing nothing but a thong and my birthday suit. It was a bit of unconventional thinking. It was unexpected, and if nothing else, it was going to surprise her.

I spent the next twenty minutes standing in the bathroom staring at myself in the mirror as I slid myself into the skimpy undergarments.

The tiger striped one wasn't going to work. It just wasn't big enough. Sections of my junk kept popping out awkwardly. It might have looked sexy if it had been intentional, but it just looked odd. A quarter profile of a single testicle isn't a very sexy thing.

I'd never been completely okay with the one with the zipper on it. My penis would shirk every time I looked at it. One wrong move and I could have found myself laying on the floor and weeping like an infant with my hands cupping my bloody crotch.

It was going to have to go with the black leather. I stepped into it and pulled it up. My ass looked like the surface of the moon if the moon had been soaked in butter and painted vampire white. The string in the rear was riding so far up my crack that it was going take a team of professional spelunkers to retrieve it. The starkness of the black made my skin seem more like zombie flesh than usual. I look like a damn fool. I looked like a complete idiot. I looked like a giant tool with an above average sized tool. *I had to do it, though. There was no turning back.*

A day later, the phone rang and I picked up. "Steven! *Ohmygod!* I'm almost home! I'm almost home!" It was my wife. She was calling from the road and she seemed excited to be on her way home. She was giggling like a Japanese woman with a plate of sushi in front of her from the original version of Iron Chef.

"Where are you?"

"I just pulled onto 12th Street! I'm almost there!!"

Crap. She was closer than I thought. I needed to get ready. "Alright sweetie. I'll see you in ten minutes."

"I love you!"

"I love you too."

The moment she hung up, I ran upstairs and snagged the thong. I dropped my britches and slid my bitches into them. (I'm not sure what "bitches" refers to in this instance, but it sounded funny. Feel free to interpret it as you see fit.)

With the barely-there string wedged deep in my crack, I headed to the workout room and proceeded to blast out a few reps in a desperate attempt to pick up just a little of my various droop. After that I jogged down the stairs and stood by the door leading into the garage.

There I was, basically naked in my kitchen at one in the afternoon. If the yard guy unexpectedly passed by the kitchen window, he was going to get an eye full of my naked ass. *Poor bastard.*

Life is weird. It's a strange, sometimes funny and sometimes royally fucked up thing, isn't it? I mean, when you really sit back and think about it, it's actually pretty ludicrous. We live and we die, and we fall in love and we fall out, and sometimes we make poor decisions—like parading our mostly disgusting bodies around in dainty underwear to impress the ones we love.

I hate life. *I love it too.*

I reached behind myself and gave my left butt cheek a little slap. I reached down below, cupped my package and give it an encouraging squeeze.

"Let's do this, big guy. Let's make her remember our name."

As luck would have it, the wife actually sort of appreciated my thong hello. She appreciated it so much that we retired to our marital bed almost immediately, where we stayed for the remainder of the day and well into the evening.

And while I'm being open and honest, she most definitely remembered my name. *Not that I'm bragging or anything.*

ABOUT THE AUTHOR

Steven Novak is a writer, illustrator, graphic designer, podcaster, and lover of all things full-blown nerdy and vaguely nerd-related. He currently resides in southern California, where he lives with his wife of over ten years. Sometimes he forgets to shave and because of this he often sports a rather shaggy beard. Goats Eat Cans Volume 2 is the second installment of an anongoing series. For more information check out **goatseatcans.blogspot.com** More of his work can be found at **novakillustration.com**